THEN AND THERE SERIES
GENERAL EDITOR
MARJORIE REEVES,

Railroads and Cowboys in the American West

BARBARA CURRIE

Illustrated from contemporary sources

LONGMAN

LONGMAN GROUP LIMITED
Longman House,
Burnt Mill, Harlow,
Essex CM20 2JE,
England

First published 1974
Sixth impression 1982
ISBN 0 582 20533 6

*Printed in Hong Kong by
Wing Tai Cheung Printing Co Ltd*

Contents

THE FIVE CENT
WIDE AWAKE
LIBRARY

Entered according to Act of Congress, in the year 1881, by FRANK TOUSEY, in the office of the Librarian of Congress, at Washington, D. C.

No. 451. { COMPLETE. } FRANK TOUSEY, PUBLISHER, 20 ROSE STREET, N. Y. { PRICE } Vol. I.
New York, August 29, 1881. ISSUED EVERY MONDAY. { 5 CENTS. }

Entered at the Post Office at New York, N. Y., as Second Class Matter.

THE TRUE LIFE OF BILLY THE KID

The legend of the Wild West began early; this five cent novel came out in 1881

To the Reader

In 1890 there was a national census in the United States. For the first time since 1790 the Census Officer did not include in his total a separate figure for people living on the frontier. There was no longer a frontier. This book tells part of the story of what is sometimes called the 'last frontier'. This was the area of the Great Plains between the Mississippi and the Rocky Mountains which previous settlers had passed over on their way to the Pacific coast. On previous frontiers there had been plenty of water and trees. The pioneer did not like the look of these vast treeless plains with rivers that dried up in summer and warlike Indian tribes on horse-back. But between 1860 and 1890 first the railroadmen, buffalo hunters and cattlemen, and then the farmers moved into the prairies, killing the game and driving the Indians into smaller and smaller reservations.

There is no shortage of books of fact about this frontier. You will find a few of them listed at the end of this book. There is no shortage of books of fiction about it either, or films, songs or poems. The real story was often as full of danger and excitement and bravery as the fiction but was not so simple or so romantic. You may have read and seen more of the legend than the fact. If you like westerns, you may be able to explain why they are so popular all over the world eighty years after the end of the frontier. Perhaps, after reading this book, you may think that the real heroes were not the lone gunmen of the films but the Chinese and Irish labourers who sweated their way across the mountains building the Union Pacific railroad or the ordinary cowboys who rode from Texas to Kansas swallowing the dust of the cattle herds or the Cheyenne soldiers who fought to the death so that their women and children could escape. Or perhaps you will think that the westerners were like most of us, a mixture of good and bad, heroic and cowardly.

Words printed in *italics* in the text are explained in the Glossary on p. 108.

1 Building the Union Pacific Railroad

Every morning at 7 o'clock
There's twenty *tarriers* a'working on the rock,
And the boss comes along and he says, 'Kape still,
And come down heavy on the cast-iron drill,
    And drill, ye tarriers, drill.

This was one of the songs of the Irish labourers who worked on the Union Pacific Railroad which was first planned in the 1850s, surveyed and laid in the 'sixties and finished in 1869.

When California and Oregon became part of the United States in the 1840s, there were already Americans living there and when gold was discovered in California in 1849, more and more people streamed westward by land and sea. By land it was a long, tough haul by wagon or on horse-back, taking months to travel across the Great Plains, over the Rockies and the Sierra Nevada to the Pacific. Look at the map on p. 20.

It did not take long for enterprising firms like Wells, Fargo and Company to start carrying *freight* by wagons or on the backs of mules over the plains and mountains, and then passengers by stagecoach. They organised the Pony Express by which relays of horses and riders carried letters on horse-back from Missouri to Sacramento, California, a distance of 1,900 miles in about ten days. When the telegraph line west was finished in 1861, this ended.

But there were already many railroads east of the Missouri and, as more settlers moved into Kansas and Nebraska, men were talking of a railroad to be built right across America from Missouri to San Francisco. Five routes were surveyed, ranging

from 48° *latitude* north near the Canadian border to 32° just

General Grenville Dodge

north of Mexico. Disputes over these routes became mixed up in the arguments which led to the Civil War between the North and the South and surveying did not begin till 1863 when the Union government in the north gave its support to the route lying about 41° north. By then a railroad had been built to within a hundred miles of Omaha, where the transcontinental railroad was to begin.

The government supported the building of the road but the actual work was done by two companies, the Union Pacific in the east, and the Central Pacific building from Sacramento to meet it. The government gave the companies a two hundred foot right of way, twenty alternate *sections* of land and loans for every mile built. It was 1,846 miles from Omaha to San Francisco.

The line had to be surveyed first. General Grenville Dodge was in charge of this for the Union Pacific. Parties of men, led 7

Surveying for the tracks. The transit man is in the centre. The flagman is not standing where he should be. Perhaps the artist did not know much about surveying

by experienced engineers and accompanied by soldiers, looked for the best route, which meant the flattest and the shortest possible. This was fairly easy on the Great Plains but in the mountains they often had to go a long way round in order to find a route with a gentle *gradient*. The government did not allow a gradient of more than 116 ft to the mile and in any case a steeper slope would make it difficult to drag the train up. The surveyors had to find passes through the mountains. Often they followed the old wagon-trails but some of these were too steep for trains. The weather along this route was very hot in summer with temperatures of over 38°C and very cold in winter, when it fell to well below −18°C. Sometimes there was so much snow that they had to give up, though the Union Pacific kept on through the desolate Wasatch mountains when they had to use sledges. The cañons of the Black Hills and the Wasatch and the steep slopes of the Sierra Nevada were especially difficult to survey and they had to clamber and climb up and down difficult cliffs.

An English doctor who went with a surveying party on the plains describes the scene as they worked:

> The men were soon spread out into line a mile long, upon the plain, measuring and taking observations at every point. On one side of this line came the wagons, following each other closely, and guarded by a small body of the escort. The remainder of the cavalry moved with the surveyors. The transit-man carrying his instrument on his shoulders and riding a mule at a gallop, would suddenly stop, jump off, arrange the transit, wave to the flag-man ahead, wait until satisfied at the correctness of his observations, then back into the saddle, shoulder his transit, and gallop away again. Behind him came the rodmen and levellers, mounted in the same way and advancing with a like rapid accuracy. It was very hard on the mules but by five o'clock that evening, fifteen miles had been chained, 'located' and levelled not by chance nor guess-work, but by an accurate preliminary survey.

The transit and level were surveyor's instruments to measure angles and the rod or chainman measured distances and marked measuring points.

The *topographers* drew maps of the district through which they passed, though under difficulties:

> Alas, sometimes after hours of toil, a gust of wind would come, upset the ink or paint-box, rip up the newly-finished map from off the impromptu table, and oblige the unfortunate map-makers to begin all their work afresh. In some places flies or grass-hoppers would insist on helping the draughtsman. Some would spot the canvas here and everywhere while others, not content with this, would first jump into the indian ink and draw maps of their own wherever they chanced to alight.

The Central Pacific surveyors followed roughly the old wagon trail from Sacramento through the Donner Pass and along the Humboldt river. The Union Pacific followed the trail up the North Platte but did not take the South Pass like the wagons because they thought it would take them too far north. Dodge encouraged his chief surveyor, James Evans, to continue searching for a new pass and he found one, Sherman Pass, further south through the Black Hills of Wyoming.

The soldiers were often in action on the Union Pacific line to protect first the surveyors and later the builders from the Indians. With the railroad builders came the hunters to provide them with meat. The hunters killed the buffalo which provided the Plains Indians with food, clothes, and tools. The Indians knew, too, that white settlers would come with the railroad and they wanted to stop it being built. There were many skirmishes between them and the soldiers, especially in 1867 when Sioux killed one of the assistant engineers and Cheyennes attacked a train at Plum Creek, killing an engine driver and a fireman. The Central Pacific did not have so much trouble with Indians, partly because the tribes on their side of the mountains were less war-like and partly because the railroad made a deal with them by which the chiefs were to have free rides on the passenger trains and the others could ride the freight trains.

After the surveyors came the graders who laid out the road-bed along the correct route, cut or blasted their way through gorges and built bridges. These were wooden trestle bridges. The graders worked well ahead of the builders, sometimes as much as a hundred miles, so that the others would not have to wait. Dodge said the track was never held up by the graders. Grading was not a safe occupation. They used gunpowder and *nitro-glycerine* to blast through the rocks which sometimes caused trouble as the song said:

> Now our new foreman was Gene McCann,
> By God, he was a blamey man.
> Last week a *premature* blast went off
> And a mile in the air went Big Jim Goff.
>   And drill, ye tarriers, drill.
> Next day when pay-day comes around,
> Jim Goff a dollar short was found;
> When asked what for, came this reply,
> 'You're docked for the time you was up in the sky'.
>   And drill, ye tarriers, drill.

When the graders had finished, the road was ready for the men to lay the track. This job was often done by contractors and sub-contractors who were paid to construct a stretch of track and hired the labourers. John and Dan Casement were the chief contractors of the Union Pacific line but some stretches were sub-contracted. When they reached Utah where the *Mormons* had settled already, Brigham Young their leader, contracted to do the grading from Echo Canon to Salt Lake for two million dollars. What with their payment of five dollars a day and ten on Sundays and selling supplies to the railroad, the Mormons did very well. The usual pay for the labourers was three dollars a day. Most of them on the Union Pacific line were Irish but Charles Crocker at the other end, used Chinese labour, 'Crocker's pets', with Irish supervisors. They were excellent workers, peaceable and hard-working, and when trained, skilled masons and blacksmiths. People thought Crocker would never train them as masons but he pointed out that the Chinese

Charles Crocker

A flat-car, wagons and workmen on the Union Pacific Railroad, 1868

had built the Great Wall of China and there wasn't a bigger piece of masonry than that. By the time the line was finished, 10,000 Chinese had worked on it.

To lay the track, the road-bed, left rough by the graders, was scraped smooth and flat. Then the gangs set in place the ties, that is the wooden cross-pieces on which the rails were laid, another gang lifted the rails from the *flat-cars* to the wagons and then they were placed in position. Gaugers saw that the rails were the right distance apart, that is 4 ft 8½ in, the 'standard' gauge. To hold the rails in position, plates were fixed in place with spikes and bolts. A journalist described the scene when the rails were laid:

> A light car, drawn by a single horse, gallops up to the front with its load of rails. Two men seize the end of a rail and start forward, the rest of the gang taking hold by twos until it is clear of the car. They come forward at the run. At a word of command the rail is dropped in its place, right side up, with care, while the same process goes on at the other side of

the car. Less than thirty seconds to a rail for each gang, and so four rails go down in a minute! Quick work, you say, but the fellows on the U.P. are tremendously in earnest. The moment the car is empty it is tipped over on the side of the track to let the next loaded car pass it, and then it is tipped back again; and it is a sight to see it go flying back for another load, propelled by a horse at full gallop at the end of sixty or eighty feet of rope, ridden by a young *Jehu*, who drives furiously. Close behind the first gang, come the gaugers, spikers and bolters, and a lively time they make of it. It is a grand Anvil Chorus that those sturdy *sledges* are playing across the plains. It is in triple time, three strokes to a spike. There are ten spikes to a rail, 400 rails to a mile, 1,800 miles to San Francisco. That's the sum. What is the answer?

Last came the men with shovels who ballasted the line, that is, filled in the space between the ties with earth and gravel.

All this equipment, as well as the men, had to be brought up to the head of the rail. They were building through land where nobody lived but Indians, miners and trappers, and that meant that all the rails, spikes and bolts had to be brought ready-made either from San Francisco or Omaha. Even before all this stuff got there, it had to come by sea to San Francisco, or at first by water or wagon to Omaha, because the connecting railroad was not finished until November 1867. The steam engine they used in Omaha was brought by wagon 143 miles from Des Moines in Iowa. Then there was food to be brought for the men, prefabricated wooden huts and tents. Even the wooden ties had to be brought in along some parts of the route. For 500 miles out of Omaha there was no wood except cottonwood which rotted too easily, and the Central Pacific had the same trouble across the Nevada and Salt Lake deserts on the other side. No wonder the bosses were angry when they found men using ties for firewood on bitterly cold nights. The prices of all these things went up fast as the railroads moved farther away from the settlements. With the railroad moved the railroad town which grew up fast at the end of the track and disappeared as fast as the road moved on. These towns were rough places. A travelling journalist described Benton, one of them:

Here had sprung up in two weeks, as if by the touch of Aladdin's lamp, a city of 3,000 people; there were regular squares arranged into five wards, a city government of mayor and aldermen, a daily paper and a volume of *ordinances* for the public health. It was the end of the freight and passenger and beginning of the construction division; twice every day immense trains arrived and departed and stages left for Utah, Montana, and Idaho; all the goods formerly hauled across the plains came here by rail and were re-shipped, and for ten hours daily the streets were thronged with motley crowds of railroadmen, Mexicans, Indians, gamblers, *'cappers'*, and saloon-keepers, merchants, miners and *bull-whackers*. The streets were eight inches deep in white dust as I entered the city of canvas tents and pole-houses, the suburbs appeared as banks of dirty white lime and a new arrival with black clothes looked like nothing so much as a cockroach struggling through a flour barrel.

He counted twenty-three saloons and five dance houses, one of them the famous 'Big Tent', a wooden and canvas building that was taken down and moved as the rail moved. While in Benton he saw an attempted *lynching*, a saloon-keeper beating his woman, a good deal of cheating in the gaming saloons and two more rows wound up the evening, 'the last ending with a perfect *fusillade* of pistol shots by which only two or three persons were 'scratched' and nobody 'pinked'. For a quiet railroad town I thought this would do and began to think of moving.'

When the town moved there was little left:

Lots in the 'wickedest' city, Julesberg, which once sold readily for a thousand dollars, are now the habitations of the owls and prairie dogs. But there is one lot in the deserted site of Julesberg whose tenants will not remove to the new railroad town. I mean the cemetery, where lie the

15

The railroad has moved on, leaving another Julesberg behind

bodies of at least a hundred victims of midnight rows, violence and *vigilantes*. The town lasted five months but was quite successful in establishing a grave-yard.'

The construction workers themselves did not have much time to whoop it up in these towns for they were too busy on their tough job—and it was tough. The Union Pacific men were building across the desert in summer when there was a shortage of water and the wind blew hot, *alkaline* dust into their faces. Later on a settler in this district talking to a visiting senator said: 'This isn't such a bad country—all it lacks is water and good society', to which the senator replied: 'Yes, that's all that hell lacks, and this part of the line was hell to the railroad builders. Farther on they were in a cold hell in the Wasatch mountains during the winter of 1868–9, 7,000 feet up, when the temperature for weeks was well below −18°C in the eating house where 'a drop of the hottest coffee spilled on the table froze in a minute, while the gravy was hard on the plate and the butter froze in spite of the fastest eater'.

The men on the Central Pacific side met the same thing but the other way round. They had to cross the mountains, the Sierra Nevada, the snowy mountains, first and then cross the hot, salt deserts. On the way from Colfax to the summit fifty miles away, at Cape Horn, the mountain was so steep that labourers had to be suspended from ropes to hack, blast and drill the road-bed, 2,500 feet above the American river. The gradients were very steep here. In twenty-eight miles the road rose 3,400 feet and for three of those miles they had to use the maximum gradients allowed by the government of 116 feet to the mile. They reached Cisco in 1867 but there was a nine months' delay while they broke a road through to the summit, where the old wagon road rose 400 feet in the mile. In fourteen miles they had to build ten tunnels, one of them 1,659 feet long. This was a particularly hard winter and they had to dig through 18 feet of snow to get to the cliff face. The forests had to be cleared of huge trees whose stumps were blasted out with gunpowder. The granite cliffs were so hard that the shot spurted out from the holes and hardly damaged the rock. They used nitro-glycerine which they manufactured in the camp, and lost some workers doing it. Because of this delay Crocker used the old wagon trail over the summit and took sleds drawn by oxen with men and supplies to the Truckee river on the other side to begin building where it was clear of snow.

Why was there all this hurry? The reason was that the money granted by the government was measured by each mile built. At first the government had said that the Central Pacific should build to the beginning of the Nevada desert but the railroad men were not satisfied with this and got a new Act passed in 1866 by which they would continue towards the Union Pacific until the two tracks met. So the last eighteen months saw a fierce race between the two companies to see who could build more track and therefore get more money.

The Union Pacific had hoped to get to Humboldt Wells at the

end of the Humboldt river but in 1868 the Central Pacific were within twenty miles of it, while the Union Pacific had only reached the Wasatch mountains east of Salt Lake. The Central Pacific hoped to get beyond Salt Lake but they had 500 miles to go, flat miles but across salt deserts where all supplies had to be brought in. They could do this more quickly than the Union Pacific could get through the Echo and Weber cañons of the Wasatch which were as difficult in their way as the Sierra, so they both reached Salt Lake at almost the same time.

Their graders met and were levelling parallel tracks along the route between Ogden and Promontory Point. The Irish at one point were on the lower road in the valley and thought it would be good fun to use dynamite without warning the Chinese above them so some of the Chinese were injured, but later on they in their turn blew up a patch of earth so that it fell on the Irish and buried them. Then they both gave it up, before the little joke cost men's lives. The government finally put an end to the race by naming Promontory Point, Utah, as the place where the two lines should meet.

Earlier on, in 1866–67, they thought they were doing well to lay two miles of track a day on flat land but as the race grew closer, these distances were stepped up to three, four, and five and then the Irish on the Union Pacific managed seven and a half miles. Charles Crocker bet that his men could manage ten if he could choose his time to do it. He did, on a flat stretch of ground with all equipment ready and when the Union Pacific men had only three miles to go so that they could not beat his record. They built the first six miles in six and a quarter hours and finished in ten. Eight rail-lifters, all Irish, lifted the thirty foot rails weighing fifty-six pounds to the yard. Calculated by the number of rails to the mile, they lifted nearly two million pounds in ten hours.

So the road was finished at last and the last spike (a golden one) was driven, at an official ceremony. The high officials of both lines, including General Dodge, came to this in two trains which drew close, engine to engine on the track. The telegraph wire had been connected to the last spike.

Driving the last spike. The lines from east to west meet at Promontory Point, Utah. Union Pacific's coal-burning locomotive N. 119 on the right; Central Pacific's wood-burning No. 60 on the left

The word was given, and 'Hats Off' went clicking over the wires to the waiting crowds at New York, Philadelphia, San Francisco, and all the principal cities. Prayer was offered, at the conclusion of which our operator tapped out: 'We have got done praying. The spike is about to be presented', to which the response came back: 'We understand. All are ready in the East.'

Four spikes were presented, two of gold and two of silver and the officials took their places.

Our operator tapped out: 'All ready now; the spike will soon be driven. The signal will be three dots for the commencement of the blows.' An instant later the silver hammer came down, and at each stroke in all the offices from San Francisco to New York, and throughout the land, the hammer of the magnet struck the bell. . . . The two engines moved up until they touched each other, and a bottle

Major Trans-Mississippi and Pacific Railroads

Line	Completed by
1 Union Pacific	1869
2 Central Pacific	1869
3 Kansas Pacific	1870
4 Denver Pacific	1871
5 Oregon Short Line	1882
6 Oregon Railway and Navigation	1883–84
7 Northern Pacific	1883
8 Denver & Rio Grande	1883
9 Texas & Pacific	1882
10 Southern Pacific	1883
11 Santa Fe	1883
11a Atlantic & Pacific	
11b Extension to Chicago	1888
12 Great Northern	1893

of champagne was poured on the last rail, after the manner of christening a ship at the launching.

In all the big cities there were celebrations, bells were rung, cannons were fired and speeches were made.

20   And so at last the Union Pacific railroad was completed.

2 More Railroads in the West

More railroads were built across the continent after the Union Pacific. Many people thought that the Union Pacific should have been built further south along the thirty-fifth *parallel* where the gradients were less steep and the winters not so cold. Union Pacific trains were sometimes held up for days or even weeks by heavy snow in the mountains. Four more railways spanned America from east to west, and they were all finished by 1893. The Southern Pacific was the furthest south, running from New Orleans to Los Angeles, keeping near the Mexican border. Furthest north was the Great Northern, built near the Canadian border. Not far south of this was the North Pacific which had many financial difficulties before it was finished. The Atchison, Topeka and Santa Fe Railroad extended its line to the Pacific (see map opposite).

All these railroads were given some kind of land grant or loan by the government, but some of the smaller lines were built by private enterprise. One of them with an exciting history of difficulties was the Denver and Rio Grande line. It was started by William Palmer with the support of Denver citizens who were discontented because the Union Pacific had by-passed them and the Kansas-Pacific took a long time to reach them. It was planned to run south to the Mexican border with branches to the mining camps in the mountains. Because the area was so mountainous, they decided to build it on a narrow 3 feet gauge, instead of the standard 4′ 8½″ gauge. People thought that this gauge took less land, and was easier to build in steep mountain country. They studied the Festiniog railway in North Wales before deciding this.

William Palmer

William Palmer had worked as a surveyor on the Kansas-Pacific but he now dreamed of a railroad of his own which would bring him profit, and also social benefits to the land. He was joined by Dr William Bell, an Englishman who had met Palmer in the surveying team. He had plans to encourage emigration to the towns planned by the railroad. It was started in 1870 and within a year they had built the line as far as Colorado Springs, the first stage, they hoped, then on to Pueblo on the Arkansas and El Paso on the Rio Grande. They reached Pueblo but another railroad, the Atchison, Topeka and Santa Fe was making towards the same area and the two companies joined battle. This was mainly a legal battle fought in the law-courts, but there were also some clashes between the men employed by the companies.

The line had to go through very narrow mountain passes, so the first to get there usually won. The Santa Fe won the race to

Raton Pass, the easiest route to New Mexico. Their chief engineer got there half an hour before the Denver men. Palmer gave up this line but he was anxious to run a branch line to Leadville, a rich silver mining centre. This had to go through the Royal Gorge of the Arkansas, a very narrow valley with steep sides. In places there was no room for two lines. The surveyors of both companies this time arrived together. While Palmer fought a battle in the courts, the companies made preparations for a battle on the site.

Block houses were built and patrols made along the line. Items like 'Arms and ammunition in April 1879, $94.50' appeared in the Denver company accounts. There was fighting in Pueblo when Palmer persuaded the sheriff to enforce an order made by the court giving his company the right to the Gorge. It was not a very big battle but a great many legends grew up around it including one that the famous gun-man from Dodge City, Bat Masterson, commanded the Santa Fe men. Palmer finally won the battle in court and built his line to Leadville but he lost out to the Santa Fe on the route to El Paso. So he built branches into the mountains to serve the mining towns finally reaching Utah and Salt Lake City. Here he came up against the Union Pacific. They tried to stop him building as far as the Union Pacific depot at Ogden, so the Denver workmen prefabricated the track and carried it forward on their shoulders to lay it under cover of a heavy rain storm. But the Union Pacific sent an engine and towed it away. So the Denver railroad laid a third track on the Union Pacific's standard gauge to carry their narrow gauge cars. The 'baby road', as it was called, was showing it had teeth. At first it had the support of the people of Utah who were tired of the Union Pacific monopoly but they found that the Denver railroad charged as much as the traffic would bear, too, so they were not much better off.

This railroad had been one of the most difficult to build, perhaps even more difficult than the Central Pacific. The mountains were so steep that they had to use a gradient of as much as 212 feet in the mile, much more than the government allowed to the railways they helped. The steep slopes and deep 23

Above: Construction work on the Denver and Rio Grande Railroad
Below left: The Denver and Rio Grande; a narrow gauge train in the Royal Gorge
Below right: An advance party in the Royal Gorge during the building of the Denver and Rio Grande in 1878-9. An incident in the war between the Rio Grande and Santa Fe railroads

gorges meant that the track was much longer than the distance covered. On the San Juan branch they built sixty-four miles of track to cover thirty-five miles and one half mile took two and a half miles of track, trestle and embankment.

Though it was so expensive and difficult to build, it was worth it to the miners who were able to transport silver much more quickly and easily. William Bell promoted settlement in the area where the railroad was built. Company towns grew up, sometimes rivalling those already there like the ones at Pueblo, Trinidad, and Durango. If they could not get good terms from the towns en route, they by-passed them and built a new town. In spite of their ideals, Palmer and Bell could be as tough and ruthless as any of the railroad builders.

Like the other roads they found it difficult to make a profit at first because they were building through new land and needed to make business for themselves. Palmer had to keep his shareholders satisfied and the companies which had received government loans and land had to pay for this.

The money came from the sale of land grants and from the passengers and freight carried by the roads. The passengers were a very mixed lot, ranging from Indians, miners and cowboys, through emigrant farming families, to rich easterners who took this fairly easy and safe way of seeing the 'wild west'. One woman passenger described the scene at Omaha as she waited for a Union Pacific train to take her west:

'Lunches put up for people going west.' This sign was put out on all corners. Piles of apparently ownerless bundles were stacked all along the platforms; but everybody was too busy to steal. Some were eating hastily, with looks of distress, as if they knew it would be long before they ate again. Others, wiser, were buying whole chickens, loaves of bread, and filling bottles with tea. Provident Germans bought sausage by the yard. German babies got bits of it to keep them quiet. Murderous looking rifles and guns, with strapped rolls of worn and muddy blankets stood here and there; murderous, but jolly-looking miners, four-fifths boots and the rest beard, strode about, keeping one eye on their weapons and bedding. Well-dressed women and men with polished shoes, whose goods were already housed in the palace-cars, lounged up and down, curious, observant, amused.

The palace cars were the Pullman cars built by the Pullman company in which a rich traveller could be very comfortable. He could have a state-room for four, a kitchen, water tanks, wine cellar and ice-box and a rich variety of food. For an emigrant farmer or a miner travelling cheap in the day-cars it was not so pleasant.

Robert Louis Stevenson, the Scottish author, travelled on an emigrant train. He compared the car to a long, narrow wooden box. It had a stove at one end and a lavatory at the other and cross-benches on each side of the central gangway. The lamps were dim and the seats were hard. At night by reversing the backs of the seats, the benches were made to face one another. The travellers could buy a board and three cushions stuffed with straw to lay across the benches. On this they slept. A newsboy travelled on the train selling books, papers, fruit, sweets and cigars. On the emigrant trains he also sold soap, towels, coffee, tea and tinned food. They could have a meal at stations but they did not know how long the train would wait, and sometimes it 'stole from the station without a note of warning and you had to keep an eye on it even when you ate'. This is why the Germans at Omaha were stocking up with sausage. Emigrant trains always had to wait for others, so they might take ten days to get from the Missouri to San Francisco, as long as the Pony Express!

The trains were apt to meet obstacles like floods, snow, broken bridges and herds of cows which could overturn an engine or car. One train was held up for eight hours on such an occasion and that could happen a hundred miles away from any settlement. They might be robbed by a gang of bandits. One Englishman was surprised by what happened when a cow was badly hurt by a train:

The conductor called out for the loan of a pistol to enable him to put it out of its misery. In an instant from every 27

The easy way to travel on the Union Pacific Railroad. A Pullman car on Sunday

window on that side of the train a hand was extended offering the desired instrument. On my making some observations on the number of pistols that were forthcoming ready loaded at a moment's notice, the gentleman seated next to me replied that it was quite possible that I was the only man unarmed on the train; in consequence of the frequent robberies no-one ever thought of moving without his six-shooter.'

Judging by the number of train robbers who were successful, not many passengers had the nerve to use their guns.

Like the passengers, freight on the line varied but in the early days of these long distance trains, the most profitable kinds of freight were the minerals from the western mines and the cattle from the Great Plains, the 'cattle kingdom' which stretched from Canada south to the Rio Grande and from the Missouri to the Rockies. The cattlemen were among the railroads' best customers.

3 Cattle Ranchers on the Great Plains

Charles Goodnight

The cattlemen were the earliest white settlers on the plains. The first big ranches were in Texas and California. Ranches in Montana were stocked from Texas cattle, later cross-bred with Herefords and Aberdeen Angus. The Texas ranchers learned from the Mexicans and the north-west cattlemen adapted their methods to suit the climate of Montana and Wyoming where the winters were long and cold.

The first cattle 'empires' on the Texas border date from before the Civil War, but Charles Goodnight is a good example of the pioneer rancher of the period after the war, trying to re-establish his business after service in the army. His first big venture, with Oliver Loving, was to drive a herd of cattle to Denver in Colorado where he hoped to sell them to the gold miners. Loving was killed by Indians on their second trail north but Goodnight started a ranch at Apishapa Cañon, forty miles north-east of Trinidad, in partnership with Loving's heirs until 1869 when he started up on his own. He was the first rancher to take a herd of cattle north to Wyoming and one of the first to settle in the Texas *Panhandle* in the Palo Duro Cañon. His description of how he dealt with the land surveyors shows how the big ranches were built up:

> I wanted that cañon. I finally got them down to *six-bits* and closed for 12,000 acres, provided that they would let me set the compass and they would run it. That is where the old Crazy Quilt comes in. I took all the good land and all the water I could get, and under the contract they were to let me *designate* 2,000 acres more that I was to take the next year at my *option*. Well, I scattered that all over the Palo Duro Canon, every good ranch in the country, every place a man was liable to come, I took.

By the crazy quilt Goodnight meant that he took patches, big patches, of land here and there wherever there was water for the cattle and good grazing, so arranged that it would be very difficult for anybody else to take the parts in between. By the *Homestead Act* Goodnight was not supposed to do this but only to take 160 acres which he could cultivate. Later Acts allowed more to people who settled in the western dry areas, if they irrigated their land and grew timber on it, but even these would not allow a cattleman the thousands of acres of open range they took. Cattle needed a lot of space and much of the land was not very suitable for small farming so the ranches took it and, as they were the first ones there, it was some time before others started to dispute their claim. 31

A ranch in New Mexico in about 1888 belonging to the Prairie Cattle Company. The trail boss is on the grey horse in the centre

Goodnight's JA ranch was 250 miles from the nearest railroad and 100 miles from his nearest neighbour, so he had to rely on himself. He was always well ahead with the latest improvements. He bought Hereford short-horn bulls to breed with his Texas long-horns. When in 1883 he added another ranch to his property, he owned 100,000 cattle and over a million acres of land, that is as much as the whole of the county of Somerset. He made his own roads and built tanks and dams for his water supply and piped water to his ranch. He had a hay farm and dairy and kept chickens. This was not common on ranches, so his buildings looked a little different from others.

Ranch buildings usually followed the same pattern, though the materials might differ. A Texas ranch might be built of *adobe*, dried mud, a Nebraska one of *sods*, while the Montana rancher had log buildings. The main house at first was very simple, usually two rooms with a space between roofed over in which saddles and other horses' gear were kept. As a rancher became more prosperous he built a better house, bringing in timber by rail if he lived on the prairies. Then there would be a separate house called a bunk-house for the cowboys and a barn with a hitching bar for the horses. There might be two or even more *corrals* for the cattle and horses. A well or a rain tank supplied the water on early ranches, but later windmills were used to work pumps. Goodnight went further and had his own blacksmith's shop, but other necessary supplies were hauled by wagon from Fort Elliott or Wichita Falls which the railroad reached in 1882.

Like all ranchers he kept open house to travellers. Unlike some, he married and his wife joined him on his frontier ranch. It was a grim life for a woman. It was said that Texas was all right for men and dogs but hell on women and horses. As one of the pioneer ranch women wrote: 'The lives of women were associated with dirt floors, dirt walls, dirt roofs, a pallet or home-made bunk for a bed, home-made furniture of all kinds, a few dishes, insufficient cooking utensils, every inconvenience of living.' In some of the semi-desert areas there could be added to that shortage of water, alkaline water which roughened the 33 skin, loneliness and, until the ranch became as prosperous as the JA ranch, poverty and fear. Most ranchers married late in life, when their ranches were in better shape for women, or their wives waited in town until they were established, but Mary Goodnight went with her husband on his first trip to the Palo Duro Cañon.

He had some trouble from Indians including Quamah Parker, the *half-breed* son of an Indian and a white woman, but he settled this without fighting. He had little trouble with cattle *rustlers* after he made an agreement with one of the best-known of them, 'Dutch Henry'. If Henry kept away from the lower Panhandle Goodnight would not bother him. Goodnight and the other ranchers kept their own law in the Panhandle as late as 1880 because there was no-one else to do it although the *Texas Rangers* sometimes came into their territory. The ranchers formed the Panhandle Stock Association to protect their property. These associations were formed throughout the cattle country and, until the homesteaders came, were all-powerful. They gave legal protection to their members, kept the official brand books, which were a record of ownership, and organised quarantine rules to stop the spread of disease. They built a two hundred mile *drift fence* north of the Canadian river to stop roaming cattle. They also arranged for the 'round-ups'.

The round-ups were held in the spring and fall to bring in and brand the calves. The most important was the beef round-up when cattle were brought in and sorted out among the various owners ready for sale. The round-up captain organised the men into groups to ride in every direction to bring in all the cattle they found. Representatives from other ranches came in to see that their own cattle were cut out from the herd and there was a stock inspector to look at the *brands*. Some associations employed special detectives at these round-ups to see that the brands had not been altered. Calves which were with their mother were easy to deal with, but calves running loose, called *mavericks*, were a problem. It was a custom for these to go to the ranch which rounded them up but this sometimes led to argu-
34 ments and the calves were an easy prey to rustlers.

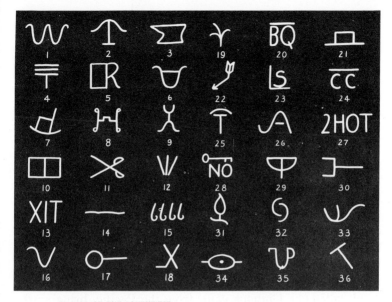

BRANDS OF THE SOUTHWEST

Some of the great brands of southwestern cattle ranching are shown above:

1. Richard King's Running W
2. Hash Knife
3. Anvil
4. Curry Comb
5. John Blocker's Block R
6. Stirrup
7. Rocking Chair
8. Spanish Bit
9. Andiron
10. Bible
11. Scissors
12. Hansford's Turkey Track
13. XIT
14. John Chisum's Long Rail
15. Burk Burnett's Four Sixes
16. Matador's Flying V
17. Glidden and Sanborn's Frying Pan
18. LX
19. Three Feathers
20. Barbeque
21. Hat
22. Broken Arrow
23. LS
24. Henry Creswell's Bar CC
25. Bugbee's Quarter Circle T
26. Goodnight and Adair's JA
27. W. E. Jackson's Too Hot
28. Cabler and Mathis' Keno
29. Captain John Rabb's Bow and Arrow
30. Driscoll's Wrench
31. Mifflin Kenedy's Laurel Leaf
32. Halff's Quien Sabe
33. Pipe
34. Hog Eye
35. Seven Up
36. Tumbling T

Brands; note the brands of ranchers mentioned in the book. The ranches were usually called after the brands (see p. 33).

The stock association not only dealt with the cattle industry but paid the local government officers like the sheriff and provided a doctor and schools, though some of the teachers were not very well qualified. Goodnight described their first one:

He was really a *roustabout*; kind of thought to be head of the thieves. He was well educated and smart as could be, so 35 when we got looking for a teacher, I said, 'Here's this son-of-a-gun! We ought to hang him. Let's put him to teaching school. We did and he made a good one too.

On the whole cattlemen did not take much interest in schooling. Granville Stuart in Montana, who was ranching at the same time as Goodnight, was different. He started a school on his own ranch and had about three thousand books in his house where some of his men got the habit of reading.

Stuart's story was rather like Goodnight's although he was ranching in very different country from the Panhandle, and started later. He staked out a claim in the Yellowstone country on the Maginnis range near the Judith mountains in 1880 and by the end of that year had 5,000 cattle. He lost some of these in the first winter when there were bad snow-storms and the temperature dropped to $-30°$ to $-40°C$. In January a warm wind called the Chinook came from the Pacific, bringing the temperature up and melting the snow. He reckoned he lost thirteen per cent of his stock, five per cent to Indians, five per cent to wild animals and three per cent to storms. Stuart had no use for the Indians who were by now on reservations. He thought they were nothing but thieves. He was a leader of the Montana Stock Growers' Association which, like the one in the Panhandle, was very powerful. They used strong methods against Indians and later against rustlers. Like Goodnight, Stuart was considered a very good employer by his men. Teddy Abbott, a cowboy who had ridden up from Texas to work in Montana, thought him the best employer he knew and he had worked for many. The 'grub' was the best he had ever tasted. 'Granville Stuart fed well, never asked his men to work too hard, took a great interest in their welfare and was always willing to help them when they were in trouble.' Abbott was perhaps a little prejudiced in Stuart's favour as he later married his daughter, Mary. By the time Abbott arrived in 1883 there were many ranchers in the same area. Abbott was given the job of representative at the spring round-ups and he had to remember forty-two
36 brands belonging to the *outfits* on the Maginnis range.

Goodnight and Stuart were individual ranchers making their own fortune but as the cattle trade became more profitable in the 1870s and 1880s, some of the land was taken up by cattle companies in which people invested just as they would in any other joint-stock company. The investors were not all Americans. Much of the money came from people in England and Scotland, and some of the managers of these ranches came from there too. John Clay was one of these and in a book about his experiences he criticised the running of these companies. Their directors in Britain 'who knew little of what was taking place around Laramie Peak or the head water of the Cheyenne river, over-estimated the profits to be made from this industry, invested too much capital and over-stocked their ranches. They were different from the early ranchers who built up these herds by economy and in the hard school of experience.' These early ranchers sometimes sold out to these companies who would often go by 'book count', that is, by the numbers of cattle stated to exist in the ranch books. When cattle ranged over thousands of acres of rough ground, the ranchers' ideas of their numbers were vague. Goodnight made himself unpopular by letting one of his best men act as counter at sales for the more cautious buyers and so spoiled the chances of cheating. Ranchers were usually honest towards each other according to their lights but considered it no sin to cheat a 'green' foreigner. By 1883 there were twenty companies with twelve million pounds capital.

There were also some amateur ranchers who came out for excitement, big game hunting or their health. A group of these settled near Medora in North Dakota in the Bad Lands. Among them were a Frenchman, the Marquis de Mores, Lincoln Lang, and Theodore Roosevelt, later President of the United States. These 'birds of passage' were regarded with some suspicion by the regular cattlemen but some of them, like these three, had a good reputation. Roosevelt's spectacles, poor physique and *dude* vocabulary did not prevent him from being accepted, as he was ready to tackle anything. A cowboy did not mind being told to 'hasten forward quickly there' instead of 'git on, git on' by someone who worked as hard as Roosevelt and the general verdict was that the 'four-eyed maverick had sand in his craw a'plenty'. These amateurs had some influence on the westerners, as they set an example of heavy investment, breeding with expensive stock, and lavish living.

The 'seventies and early 'eighties were the heyday of the cattlemen. Sales were good, profits were high and loans were easy to come by from the western banks which had often been started by the cattlemen themselves. The most prosperous of them were living 'high off the hog', as they would say themselves, and even a working cowboy might hope to save up enough to buy a few cattle and start off as Stuart and Goodnight had done. The cattlemen were the organisers and capitalists of the industry but the cowboys, 'as the common labourers were called', did the day-to-day work and it is time for us to see what working with cattle meant.

Theodore Roosevelt; the 'four-eyed maverick'

4 Learning to be a Texas Cowboy

A Texas long-horn; the kind of cattle James Cook hunted in the brush and drove north to Texas

When James Cook left his home in Michigan in 1873, first for Kansas and then for Texas, he was sixteen. He described how his life as a cowboy began:

> I went to south-western Texas with some cowboys who had brought a herd of cattle up from that country to Kansas, and who were then about to make a return journey. I had purchased a fine Comanche pony at Fort Harker for $15 and a good second-hand Texas saddle for $5.00. I had traded a pistol brought from Michigan for a Spencer *carbine*, and was therefore fixed for the journey.

39

He was hired by Ben Slaughter, a well-known Texan cattle-man, to catch wild cattle in the land between the Nueces River and the Rio Grande. This was brush country. The land was covered with trees with low-hanging branches and masses of thick undergrowth. Most of these bushes and trees had thorns, like the mesquite and the chaparral which sometimes spread over hundreds of acres, or the junio, the 'all-thorn', or the coma with thorns like daggers. All these plants could stand up to drought in the hot Texas summer and so spread rapidly.

When Cook went to Texas the brush still swarmed with wild cattle, the Texas longhorns, descendants of the cattle brought by the Mexicans into Texas. These had multiplied and run wild over the wide ranges, especially since the Civil War when there were few men to guard them and nowhere to take them to market. The horns of these cattle could be four feet across, they were long-legged, lean and fierce. Cowboys never went near them on foot, except to brand them and then they had someone nearby on a horse in case a *steer* broke loose.

Before going to catch the cattle Slaughter's men rounded up a small herd of tame cattle as *decoys*. These would be used to attract the wild cattle and mix with them to calm them down. They also made *hobbles* for the horses.

> This was new work for me, but it was not many months before I would work up raw-hide into saddle rigging, ropes, *quirts* and reins, doing all sorts of knot tying and braiding and plaiting. My Mexican instructors were all very kind to me.

When the cattle hunt began, Cook found that he needed special equipment and clothing for the job: a thick canvas jacket like the Mexicans with whom he worked, heavy leather leggings or *chaparejos*, gauntleted gloves, a wide-brimmed hat with a chin-strap, high heeled boots to hook firmly into the stirrups which themselves had leather toe-fenders. This clothing which the Mexican *vaqueros* wore was copied by the Texans who, in turn, were copied by the cowboys of Montana and Wyoming whom they met when they drove cattle north.

A young Texas cowboy; not James Cook, but dressed like him and riding the same kind of cow-pony

Cook's description of his first hunt in the brush shows why he needed all this. A small herd was found and they gave chase:

I gave my horse the reins, trailing the ones ahead by the crashing of limbs and dead brush. I was kept pretty busy dodging the limbs which were large enough to knock me from the saddle or warding the smaller limbs and brush from my face with my arm. I think I rode all over that pony – first on one side, then on the other, then as he dived under some big live-oak limb almost under his neck. We crossed several prickly-pear patches where the clumps grew from two to ten feet high and about as close together as they could stand. My pony would jump over, knock down or run through any of them. He was a cow-catcher by trade. He certainly made me 'pull leather', and I clung to his mane as well in order to keep in close touch with him. My clothing was pretty well torn off, also a goodly portion of my skin. About nine kinds of thorn were imbedded in my anatomy.

The cow-ponies were small compared with the saddle horses of the east, but very tough and hardy, living like the cattle on wild grass or anything else they could forage. When trained they knew their job better than a beginner like Cook and could weave and dodge and turn on a *dime* and leave some change – or so their owners claimed. They were much wilder than eastern horses. The first one Cook saddled 'jumped in the air and tried to turn cartwheels' and even the best trained were not easy to saddle. Cowboys placed great value on a good pony and were very unwilling to part with it. Sometimes when the ponies died or were killed, they were given an epitaph like:

Jim
a reel hors
Oct. '82

Cook was too inexperienced to use a rope on his first hunt but every cowboy carried a *lasso* or *lariat*. In the brush they used a short twenty-five feet rope as the thirty to forty feet ones used on the open plains were useless. The rope was carried coiled on the horn of the high western saddle and tied to it in the brush country where it was hard to keep hold of a rope. Cook once lost rope, saddle and all, and went over the horse's head when his saddle girth snapped after he had roped a bull. It was dangerous, too, if a roped steer ran round the other side of a tree.

Any boy who grew up in cattle country could use a rope. As children they roped anything, the gate-posts, hens, calves, dogs and each other. An adult cowboy never lost the habit and would try to rope a buffalo–though only young ones if he had any sense–or anything that moved. One folk-song even tells the story of two drunken cowboys on their way home who roped, tied and branded the Devil when he stopped them to claim their sinful souls.

They did not always rope cattle round the horns but sometimes round the hind- or fore-legs. A very skilled man could make a figure of eight with his rope and catch both legs in it. There was another way of throwing a steer which Cook describes.

> Failing because of thick timber or bothersome brush, to get his rope on an animal, he had just one chance left; to spur his horse alongside the fleeing beast, catch it by the tail with his hand and, taking a turn around a saddle horn, dash suddenly ahead, causing the steer to turn a somersault.

This could break the steer's neck–or, of course, the cowboy's if he failed. As one observer remarked, a cattle ranch was no place for a member of the Humane Society.

The cowboys, besides horses and ropes, needed knives for skinning dead cattle, cutting ropes if necessary, eating their food and sometimes in a fight. Cook bought a knife in a pawnshop in San Antonio, 'a very fancy *bowie knife* of great weight. On its blade was engraved this inscription: "Never draw me without cause, never sheathe me without honor."' More experienced cowboys than Cook went in for fancy equipment in the way of fine saddles, harness, boots, belts and hat straps, though they were content with dark trousers and shirts. Their *bandana* handkerchiefs might be brightly coloured to begin 43 with, though not after they had been used as masks against hail or sand-storms, as emergency bandages, towels or a dozen other things.

Some cowboys carried a gun, used more for shooting maimed, diseased or dangerous cattle than each other, or for firing into the air in celebrations. Since a Colt .45 weighed two and a quarter pounds, they did not carry one unless they had to and very rarely carried two. For the same reason they did not carry a rifle unless they were hunting or in danger from an Indian attack. The weight of it in its *holster* on one side of the saddle could upset the balance and rub sores in the horse's skin.

When a bunch of wild cattle had been rounded up, they were herded close to the decoy cattle, and then driven to a corral. These were enclosures with timber fences seven or more feet high, made of poles lashed together with green cow-hide. As this dried it shrank, pulling the posts closer together. The gate posts were strong with bar poles slung between them. From the gate posts two long fences, sometimes two hundred yards long, spread out at an angle to make a V-shaped entrance, tunnelling the cattle towards the gate.

When the cattle had quietened down they were roped, thrown and branded. Two cowboys would rope the steer, one round the horns and one round the leg, then two flankers would throw it down, hobble and hold it while another branded it. For this the men used either a running iron, a red-hot poker used rather like a pencil to trace the brand, or an iron on which the whole brand had been engraved so that it was applied all at once. Each owner had a brand which was registered and checked by inspectors but brands could be altered fairly easily by a running iron. Later on any cowboy who carried a running iron might be suspected of being a rustler.

Cook's description of his first ride justifies the definition of a cowboy as a man 'with guts and a horse'. If they lost their nerve they had to give up, as some did. Most of them were young men like Cook. Many died in accidents or fights. One rancher said that an old cowboy was as scarce as hen's teeth. If they were
44 not 'rubbed out' young, they usually went on to other jobs or

became cattle owners themselves if they saved up enough, as Cook did when he was older.

Cook got $10 a month and board to start with, two dollars more than the Mexicans, but an experienced American rider could get $25 or a top rider $30–40 or even double this if he were a foreman. 'Board' meant food and a bunk when working on the ranch or when away in camp a couple of blankets or a Tucson bed, that is 'you lie on your stomach and cover it with your back'. Food and the equipment for cooking and eating it was simple:

> We used pack mules and ponies for carrying our provisions and cooking utensils. Our provisions consisted of green-berry coffee, salt side of pork, corn-meal, *saleratus*, salt and pepper berry. Our cooking utensils and dishes consisted of a couple of *Dutch ovens*, a frying pan, a camp kettle or two and a coffeepot. We had each a tin cup holding about a pint, together with a tin plate and an iron knife and fork. Sugar was not furnished us. Our pack train generally carried a plentiful supply of black navy plug tobacco and some pre-pared corn-husks for cigarette wrappers. Matches were very scarce in that country and each man carried a flint and steel, together with a piece of *punk* or prepared cotton tape with which to build fires or 'make a smoke'.

More was added to this on long expeditions when a *chuck-wagon* was taken, but even then the extra was only bacon, sourdough biscuits, *molasses* and a little dried fruit.

Because there were no fences on the ranges, it was easy for cattle to drift away and sometimes the cowboys were away from the ranch buildings line-riding, when they camped in the open or lived in a small wooden or sod hut. Starting miles apart they rode along the approximate boundary line of the ranch towards each other then met and turned. They drove back straying cattle onto their boss's land, and helped cattle which were injured, bogged down or in any other difficulties, especially the motherless calves, the dogies.

Cook learned all a cowboy's jobs on Slaughter's ranch but he 45

Roping a calf, 1907. By then, the old long-horns had been crossed with Herefords

Branding calves in the Cherokee strip, 1889

BRANDING CALVES

did not stay long. He did not get on well with the foreman and, like most cowboys, he had the itch to move on and try somewhere else, so he signed up to drive cattle north to Abilene in Kansas. When he applied to Joe Roberts, the foreman for the job, Roberts said:

> They tell me you can catch a cow and shoot a rabbit's eye out every pop. Now if you can ride for the next four months without a whole night's sleep, and will turn a gun loose on any damned Indian who tries to get our horses, why, git ready. We will roll out tomorrow.

These were the qualifications for employment on a cattle trail.

James Cook; a photograph taken after he had given up cow-punching for hunting

5 Pointing them North

James Cook was starting on a well-beaten trail when he set out to Kansas in 1873. Before the Civil War, cattle had been trailed from Texas to California, Louisiana and the north. Because of conditions after the war this practice had grown more common. Texas had been part of the Southern *Confederacy* during the war and had been cut off from the northern markets. The stock had multiplied by thousands and scattered through the southern ranges but there was nowhere to sell the cattle. The railroads had not reached Texas and the Gulf ports could take little. In 1866, you remember, Charles Goodnight and Oliver Loving had taken a herd up the Pecos to Denver to the miners, along the trail later called after them, but the first big drives were to Kansas because the railroad had reached there by 1866.

In Kansas, a businessman called Joseph McCoy had made a deal with the U.P., Hannibal and St Joseph railroad company to ship cattle back to Chicago. He established his headquarters at Abilene, the first of the cow towns. As time went on, Wichita, Ellsworth, Dodge City in Kansas, Ogallala in Nebraska and Cheyenne in Wyoming also became *termini* for the cattle drovers who were taking cattle to the railheads, the northern ranges or the Indian reservations. The trails were given names like the Shawnee, the Western, and the Chisholm. The first drive to Kansas was in 1867 and between then and 1880 over four million cattle were driven north to Kansas. The cattlemen had a plan after that for one national trail, but by then the cattle industry was declining, so it came to nothing.

The trails were wide beaten tracks following the easiest routes north, pioneered by the first herds and followed by the others.

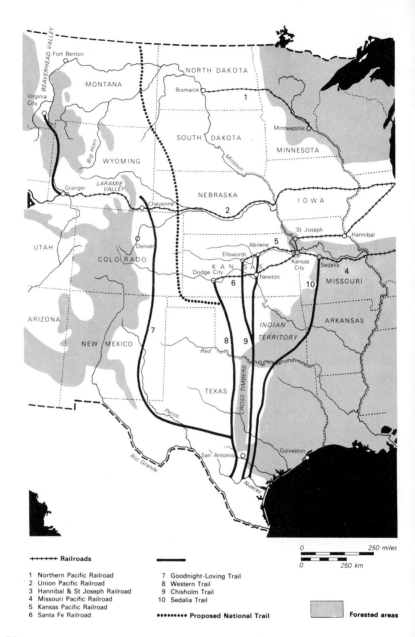

+++++ **Railroads**

1 Northern Pacific Railroad
2 Union Pacific Railroad
3 Hannibal & St Joseph Railroad
4 Missouri Pacific Railroad
5 Kansas Pacific Railroad
6 Santa Fe Railroad

7 Goodnight-Loving Trail
8 Western Trail
9 Chisholm Trail
10 Sedalia Trail

●●●●●●● **Proposed National Trail**

Forested areas

Joseph McCoy

There were usually between two and three thousand cattle in a herd with a trail crew of twelve riders, with a cook and a boy. The youngest boy was often the wrangler, that is he was in charge of the horse herd or *remuda*. A popular cowboy song told the story of little Joe the wrangler, a runaway, who was given a job as a horse herder by a kindly boss who:

> Learned him to wrangle horses and to know them all
> To get them in at daybreak if he could,
> To follow the chuck wagon and always hitch the team
> And help the *cocinero* gather wood.

James Cook had this job but he helped with the cattle herding as well. The men's equipment was the same as that used for the cow-hunts on the Nueces but on the later trails there was a chuck-wagon driven by the cook. The cowboys' bed-rolls were loaded on this and the food and cooking equip- 51

Cowboys riding towards the chuck-wagon

Left: *Chuck-wagon; same kind of wagon, pans and equipment as in 1880 but a much later photograph. How can you tell?*

ment carried in the chuck-box at the back. This wagon, with the remuda, went on ahead of the herd. The trail boss was well in the lead. His job was to 'ride his tail off' looking for a suitable trail through the brush, the deserts, the *gulches* and the plains of the twelve hundred miles between Texas and Kansas, and finding a good place for the herd to bed down at night. One of his chief problems was water. He must be sure that the herd did not take too long a drive without water. This was not always possible on a dry drive of sixty or a hundred miles, like that across the Staked Plain from the South Concho to the Pecos. Too much water could also be a difficulty and the boss must find easy crossing places on rivers swollen by heavy rain.

Some miles behind the boss the herd would be strung out in a long narrow line stretching half a mile. At the head rode the 53

Holding a 'sun-fisher', a rearing horse, Arizona

two pointers who guided the cattle, never allowing them to break into a trot. Some cowmen used a lead steer which always kept ahead. Charles Goodnight's 'Old Blue' was a famous steer which led one or two drives a year for eight years, his brass bell tinkling in the lead. He was canny enough to keep out of stampedes and trouble. He became a pet of the cowboys and lived to be twenty. On each side behind the pointers were the swing men and behind them the flank riders. At the rear were the drag men who prodded the laggards, went after strays and shot injured cattle. The pointers were always the same men but the others took turns at the different jobs so that nobody spent all his time swallowing the dust in the drag. They kept the cattle at a steady, ambling walk which did not prevent them snatching an odd mouthful of grass as they went along. There was no point in rushing them, especially after the buyers in Kansas started to buy them by the pound instead of by the head. Lean, tough cattle would not fetch much so they usually averaged a 54 steady ten to twelve miles a day.

A herd on the trail; above: *pointers at the front,* below: *riding in the drag*

On a good day they walked from first light to dusk, a whole day in the saddle for the men, coated with dust and sweating in the hot sun. At night the chuck wagon stopped, its tongue pointing to the North Star in strange country, and the cook started preparing supper. After watering at the stream or ponds (if any), the lead cattle were turned in a curve so that the cattle formed a circular herd and then they bedded down for the night. When the cook had the meal ready, the first watch ate, then caught fresh horses and returned to ride round the herd while the second and third watch ate and slept. They knew when to change guard by watching the Great Dipper. The Dipper swings round the North Star every twenty-four hours. The men on the first watch noted the position of the pointer or hands in relation to the North Star and changed guard when the hands marked off one third of the night.

The guards rode slowly round and round the herd crooning the Texas lullaby. This was a monotonous, crooning song, sometimes wordless, sometimes with words, about the cowboy's work and life. For some reason this calmed the cattle which were often restless at night so that the howl of a *coyote* or the flash of lightning would set them off on a stampede. The tunes were old folk tunes, popular songs and hymn tunes, but the words were often about the cowboy's job like one of the best known, 'Git along little *dogies*'.

As I walked out one bright summer morning
I met a gay cowboy come ridin' along,
His hat throwed back and his spurs was a-jinglin',
As I approached him, he was singin' this song.
  A hoop-an-i-hay, go on, you little dogies,
  O hoop-an-i-hay, Wyomin's your home.
Now some boys tries the trail for pleasure,
But them that does gits it awfully wrong,
You never see the like of the trouble they give us,
While we roll those longhorn cattle along.

You're gonna make beefsteak for *Uncle Sam's Injuns*,
'It's beef, heap beef, I hear them call,'

Roll on, roll on, roll on, you damn dogies,
You're gonna be beefsteak long before fall.

You was born and raised below the Nueves,
Where the mesquite and cactus and chaparral grow
So fill yourselves up with grass in Kansas
And roll your tails for old Idaho.
It's whoopin' and cussin' an' damning those dogies
To our souls' perdition but none of their own.

Next morning the cowboy would be up for a four o'clock break-fast and start the cattle on the trail again.

But not all the days were good days and the cowboys might face many dangers and difficulties. It did not do to become ill. 'Should anyone become injured, wounded or sick he would be strictly out of luck. A quick recovery and a sudden death were the only desirable alternatives in such cases.' Injuries could come from attacks by cattle. In the rivers they sometimes became bogged down in mud or quicksand and had to be dragged out with ropes. They often then ungratefully attacked their rescuers. An 'outlaw' steer was liable to turn on a man at any time. The greatest danger of injury or death was in a stam-pede. Cook's herd stampeded on their first night out, a stam-pede that Cook had caused, though he kept quiet about it at the time. An old cow was lying fifty yards from the herd and, to see how near he could go to her as he rode round, he touched her and she plunged into the herd starting them all off. Thunder and lightning could cause a stampede and there were tremen-dous thunder storms on the prairies.

Once the cattle started running they were very hard to stop, especially as the night might be dark and the ground cut up by wind *erosion* and water and criss-crossed by gulches up to twenty-five feet deep. Cook saw many stampedes:

To stay with them we had to ride as fast as a horse could run. Sometimes it would be so dark that a rider could not see his horse's head. Then a flash of lightning would come and we could see the cattle tearing madly along and locate the 57 position. The next moment one would again be blinded by the flash. Many were the hard falls the boys had to take when a horse went down while running after stampeded stock on those dark and stormy nights. Many were the poor old 'leather-breeches' who came dragging themselves into camp the morning after a bad night, either with broken bones or carrying their saddles on their backs, because their horses had fallen and broken a neck or a leg. And I know personally a few of the boys who had to be left by the side of the long trail to wait for the call of the great trumpeter Gabriel, because of those terrible runs at night.

One of the boys was a young partner of Cook's killed going over the edge of a gulch with a bunch of cattle. The little wrangler of the song came to the same end:

> Next morning just at sun-up we found where Rocket fell
> Down in a *wash-out* twenty feet below,
> Beneath his horse smashed to a pulp, the spurs had rung
> the knell,
> Was our little Texas stray, poor wrangler Joe.

On Cook's second trail, a *tornado* started the cattle off.

> I have never seen such queer-looking clouds before. They seemed to be rushing toward the centre of the heavens and we could hear a steady, sullen roar which seemed to come from every direction. We hastily staked the wagons to the ground as tightly as possible and lashed the wagon sheet down with extra rope.

The horses stampeded and some fell down a gulch. Cook's horse got away and he had to walk knee deep in hail-stones. The trees by the river were torn out by the roots,

> thousands of prairie dogs and little prairie dog-owls as well as rabbits and rattlesnakes, had been drowned out of their holes and chilled or beaten to death by hail. Even the grass was smashed off at the roots and washed away in drifts of hail.

Above: *A stampeding herd*
Below: *Herd swimming the river; a cowboy ahead*

A. CAS

They managed to get most of the horses and cattle back, but it was no wonder that no company would insure a cowboy's life.

If the trail-drivers started too early in the spring, snow and ice were a hazard. In 1874 a year after Cook's first trip, a whole remuda was frozen to death at Hell Roaring Creek in Indian Territory. Melting snow led to deep, fast-flowing rivers. Many drowned swimming their horses across the rivers. One cattle driver kept a diary in which he described the four days he spent at the Brazos during an especially wet spring:

MAY 14   Concluded to Cross Brazos swam our cattle and Horses and built Raft & Rafted our provisions and blankets etc. over Swam river with rope and then hauled wagons over lost Most of our Kitchen furniture such as camp kittles Coffee Pots Cups Plates Canteens etc. etc.

MAY 15   back at River bringing up wagon hunting Oxen and other lost property Rain poured down for one Hour. It does nothing but rain got all our traps together that was not lost and thought we were ready for off dark rainy night cattle all left us and in morning not one Beef to be seen.

The end of the trail for one cowboy; a cowboy's funeral

MAY 16   Hunt Beeves is the work—all Hands discouraged and are determined to go 200 beeves and nothing to eat.

MAY 17   No Breakfast pack and off is the order. all Hands gave the Brazos one good harty dam and started for Buchanan.

Winds, dust-storms and prairie fires might be just as much danger as too much water. The early trails to Kansas passed over Indian Territory, roughly present-day Oklahoma, to which several Indian tribes like the Cherokees and Creeks had been moved by the government. They were allowed to claim 'duty' on cattle going through their territory but they often begged for cattle or stole them. Indians like the Comanches who were not 'settled' often drove cattle off. This happened to Cook on his first trail when the Comanches shot and wounded the horse guard who had just relieved Cook and stampeded horses and cattle through the camp. They managed to hold the cattle a half a mile away but lost some of the horses. Cook and two others, with some buffalo hunters whose horses had been stolen too, followed the Indians, attacked their camp and recovered some of the horses.

If they got to the Kansas border safely there was one last difficulty. Texas cattle often had an infectious disease called Texas fever which did them little harm but infected the tamer cattle of the Kansas settlers. These farmers wanted a quarantine law to keep the cattlemen from driving across their land to the railroad. This was passed, but the drovers often got round it, encouraged by the people who ran the cow-towns which lived off the cattle trade. But the farmers sometimes enforced the law themselves by driving off the cattle and attacking the cowboys.

For the cowboy, the trail meant three months of these dangers, sheer hard work, little sleep and rough food. Most of the cattlemen would not allow alcohol on the drives and some forbade card-playing as well. One went further and rested the herds on Sundays and forbade drinking, cards, gambling and swearing. But they had fun when they had the time to spare, as one said:

> After supper the boys not on herd would tell yarns, sing songs, wrestle and act generally like a bunch of kids which mostly we were. Like many of the outfits ours had a fiddle, and while some artist in spurs 'made it talk' we often put the end gate of the chuck wagon on the ground and took turns dancing jigs on it.

James Cook sometimes enjoyed the work itself.

> When the weather was fine and we had plenty of rest and food, I enjoyed cowboy life thoroughly and at such times I would not have exchanged places with the Prince of Wales. . . . On beautiful warm moonlight nights when I was riding around those immense herds, I would say to myself, 'This is the life.'

They felt the same when they reached the end of the trail and had a splendid spree in Abilene.

6 The Cattle Towns

Abilene, Kansas; the end of the trail

Like the railroad towns the cattle towns had a rough reputation, sometimes earned, sometimes exaggerated. They owed their existence to the railroads and the cattlemen. When the drives moved farther west, they became small farming towns. Joseph McCoy described Abilene in 1867 as:

> A very small, dead, place, consisting of about a dozen log huts—low, small, rude affairs, four-fifths of which were covered with dirt for roofing; indeed but one single shingle roof could be seen in the whole city. The business of the burg was conducted in two small rooms, mere log-huts, and of course the inevitable saloon, also in a log hut, was to be found.

For five years Abilene boomed as a terminus of the cattle drives and then the more sober citizens asked the cattlemen to take the cattle to other railhead towns like Ellsworth and Wichita.

Joseph McCoy built the Drover's Cottage, a big hotel with a hundred rooms, a laundry, a dining room and a verandah. Here the cattlemen stayed and made their bargains with McCoy. The main street running east to west was called Texas street, and the biggest saloon was called the Alamo after the famous battle which the Texans had fought against the Mexicans back in 1836. The Alamo had a long bar backed by a mirror while the walls were covered with huge cheap imitations of *Renaissance* paintings of nude women. Here the customers would drink, gamble, dance or listen to the saloon's own orchestra. Cowboy dancing was more energetic than elegant. Joseph McCoy described it:

> With the front of his sombrero lifted at an angle of fully forty five degrees, his huge spurs jingling at every step or motion, his revolvers flapping up and down, his eyes lit up with excitement, liquor and lust, he plunges in and 'hoes it down' at a terrible rate in the most approved yet awkward country style, often swinging his partner clear off the floor for an entire circle, then 'balance all' with an occasional demoniacal yell near akin to the war-whoop of the savage Indian. After dancing furiously the entire 'set' is called to 'waltz to the bar' where the boy is required to treat his partner and, of course, himself also; which he does not hesitate to do time and time again, although it costs him fifty cents each time.

James Cook was one of the quieter ones, so Teddy Abbott, another young cowboy, is a better guide to the pleasures of the end of the trail. He regularly spent all his money as soon as he had it until his girl-friend, Mary Stuart, refused to marry him unless he saved some money and settled down. He said, 'When they hit the bright lights of some little cow-town that looked like gay Paree to them, they just went crazy.' First they wanted 64 –and needed after three months on the trail–a bath, then hot

Above: *Dance hall in Abilene; 'hoeing it down'*
Below: *A saloon in Clovis, New Mexico*

food. 'Do you know what was the first thing a cow puncher ordered to eat when he got to town? Oysters and celery. And eggs. Those things were what he didn't get and what he was crazy for.'

Then they would go off to buy new clothes:

> I had a new white *Stetson* hat that I paid ten dollars for and new pants that cost twelve dollars, and a good shirt and fancy boots. They had colored tops, red and blue, with a half-moon and a star on them. Lord, I was proud of those clothes! They were the kind of clothes top hands wore, and I thought I was dressed right for the first time in my life.

The general stores in these towns had a large stock:

> Anything or Everything from a paper of pins to a Portable House, Groceries, Provisions for your camp, ranch or farm; Clothing, Hats, Caps, Boots and Shoes, Underclothing, Overalls and all kinds of furnishing goods; Studebaker Wagons, the best in the market, a Genuine California or Texas Saddle, a Nobby Side Saddle, A Sett of Harness, a rifle, carbine, pistol or festive Bowie knife, Camp Equippage of any kind, a full assortment of Building Hardware.

After shopping came drinking, dancing, singing, gambling, and a visit to the theatre if there was one. They were not the quietest audience in the world. Abbott went to a play in Denver, in which a burglar beat his wife to death. The noise of this woke one of the cowboys who had been asleep.

> He gave one jump onto the stage and busted the fellow on the head with his six-gun before he remembered where he was. The woman got up and began to cuss him, all hell broke loose, somebody pulled Bill off the stage, they called the police, the boys shot out the lights, and everybody broke their necks getting away from there.

Abbott was a great one for singing. One of his favourites was 66 'The Streets of Laredo'.

Dodge City, the all-important railroad line in the foreground

As I rode out by Tom Sherman's bar-room,
As I rode out so early one day,
'Twas there I espied a handsome young cowboy,
All dressed in white linen and all clothed for the grave.

'I see by your outfit that you are a cowboy'
These words he did say as I boldly stepped by
'Come sit down beside me and hear my sad story
For I'm shot in the breast and I know I must die.'

'Twas once in the saddle I used to go dashing,
'Twas once in the saddle I used to go gay,
But I first took to drinking and then to card-playing
Got shot in the breast and I'm dying today.

'Let sixteen gamblers come handle my coffin,
Sixteen young cowboys come sing me a song,
Take me to the green valley and lay the sod o'er me,
For I'm a poor cowboy and I know I've done wrong'.

Abbott said,

I first took to drinking and then to card-playing—and they'd
be drunk even when they were singing it most likely. Cowboys used to love to sing about people dying; I don' know
why. I guess it was because they were so full of life themselves.

67

Another favourite, 'Bury me not on the lone prairie' they sang to death.

> It was a saying on the range that even the horses nickered it and the coyotes howled it; it got so they'd throw you in the creek if you sang it. I first heard it along about '81 and '82 and by '85 it was prohibited.

Most of the cowboys gambled; there was plenty of opportunity in the saloons where they could play *monte, faro, seven-up, poker* and many other games. The gamblers were not always honest, so there was rather a high death and injury rate among them. Many cowboys spent all they'd got for pay or gambled it away and went back to Texas 'cleaned out'.

After 1872 fewer and fewer cattle came to Abilene, as the country around attracted more settlers and *homesteaders* who did not want wild Texas cattle over their land and as Abilene citizens wanted more churches and schools and less saloons and dance halls. First they moved these to a separate part of the town and then they asked the cattlemen not to come again. So they went to other towns. With them went the traders, the hotel keepers and the gamblers and prostitutes to another town which in turn had the same bad reputation. Sometimes the buildings went too. The Drover's Cottage was taken down, packed up and moved on to Ellsworth. One grocer moved first to Ellsworth and then to Wichita. The last of the Kansas towns to boom was Dodge City, claimed to be the worst. The story goes that a drunken cowboy getting on the train at Newton gave the rail-roadman a fistful of money. 'Where to?' the man asked. 'To hell,' said the cowboy. 'Well just give me $2.50 and get off at Dodge.' It was true that out of the forty-five people killed in the five Kansas cowtowns between 1870 and 1885, Dodge accounted for fifteen, but at an average of three a year that compares quite well with some modern towns. James Cook reckoned that the automobile killed, scalped and maimed more people than ever the Indians did and that the old West was safer to live in. There was more law and order in the towns than the story-writers would admit.

7 Law and Order on the Frontier

The drinking and sky-larking of the cowboys, the cheating of the gamblers and arguments with buffalo-hunters and soldiers often led to fighting with knives or guns either between two men or a free-for-all. Their aim was not particularly good as they were usually too drunk to see straight and they often injured by-standers. Texas cowboys did not often fight with their fists; they considered this beneath them. Texans were inclined to hang together especially in the north as many of them were ex-Confederate soldiers from the Civil War and even a reference to *Dixie* from a northerner was apt to start a fight.

In Abilene a jail was one of the early buildings, not as early as it might have been because the cowboys tore it down while it was under construction. They also rescued the first prisoner in it, a Negro cook from a nearby cow-camp. As more permanent residents moved in, a Board of Trustees was appointed and then in 1871 a Mayor and Council were elected. They made regula-tions, including a rule that no fire-arms were to be carried but the notice-board announcing this was shot full of holes. Then they appointed their first town marshal, Tom Smith. He had kept order in the railroad towns on the Union Pacific and proved to be one of the most successful marshals of the Kansas cow-towns. He was paid $150 a month. He first tried to enforce the regulation about guns. One cowboy refused to give his up, so Smith hit him and took his gun away. Another challenged him so he hit him too, took his gun, beat him over the head with it and told him to leave town. This happened in a saloon. The proprietor handed over his gun and Smith did not have much difficulty in making men obey this rule from then on. He 69

Tom Smith; first marshal of Abilene

Wild Bill Hickok, second marshal of Abilene. He liked to dress up in 'wild west' style for the photographer

patrolled along the centre of the streets regularly on horse-back, keeping an eye open for trouble-makers. He was not marshal for long because he was killed by two homesteaders when he went to arrest them.

His successor, 'Wild Bill' Hickok was famous as a gun-man, though much of his fame came from a very inaccurate article about him in a well-known magazine. Like many of the gun-fighters of Kansas, Hickok had fought in Kansas before the Civil War, when pro-slavery and anti-slavery men were fighting for possession of the territory, and then during the War. Much of the border fighting in Kansas and Missouri had been 'guerrilla' warfare in which a good deal of looting and raiding took place which did not have much connection with the main campaigns. Besides Hickok, 'Buffalo Bill' Cody, Jesse James, the Younger brothers and many others had fought on one side or the other. Hickok had been a wagon-master and guide since the war, and had been tried for murder and acquitted. Many people thought he was a poor marshal compared to Smith. He joined in the gambling and drinking and spent much of his time in the Alamo saloon, not patrolling the streets like Smith. His reputation as a gunman helped to protect him. While in Abilene he shot and killed two men in a fight. One of them was his own policeman whom he shot by mistake. The Abilene Council dismissed him after a year and he drifted on to other jobs, including acting in Buffalo Bill's Wild West show, before being shot in the back in Deadwood.

Most of the cow-towns had a marshal with one or two policemen and more during the trail-driving season. Besides keeping order, they were expected to remove obstructions and keep stray animals off the streets and keep the side-walks repaired. Some of the lawmen were chosen from possible trouble-makers, perhaps on the principle of setting a thief to catch a thief. Some of them, like Hickok, had been in trouble for breaking the law and a marshal in Caldwell was caught robbing a bank in a neighbouring town. The officials in Dodge City came under this heading. Some of the trouble in the cow-towns arose because of quarrels between rival groups in local government which later might be settled by votes and discussions but tended to become violent when men carried guns. This happened in Dodge City in the 1880s when one group elected their candidate to be Mayor and they started their reforms by fining women in the saloons belonging to the rival group. The Dodge City 'war' which followed did not lead to many casualties, even though one group was supported by Bat Masterson, Wyatt Earp and other gunmen. The newspapers forecast trouble but the two groups settled their quarrel without bloodshed.

Besides the town marshals and policemen, order was kept by the elected sheriffs of the counties, who could call on all able-bodied men to help him form a *posse*. The government in Washington appointed federal marshals in the *Territories* or to catch criminals who crossed State boundaries. If there was danger of general fighting the *militia* might be called out. This was a citizen army of volunteers, more often used for fighting

Indians than keeping order. Federal soldiers might be used in serious situations like the Johnson County War which you will hear about later. Texas had its own body of police, the Texas Rangers, and many of the railroads and banks employed private detectives, sometimes from the famous firm of Alan Pinkerton. In the early days of a territory with no established law, groups of 'vigilantes' often took the law into their own hands. These were local people who hunted down rustlers and bandits and hanged them, without bothering much about trials or evidence. This was the case in Montana where the sheriff was found to be a leader of a gang of highwaymen. Granville Stuart was one of the leaders of this vigilante movement and people who disapproved called them 'Stuart's stranglers'.

Lynchings like this often did happen but law-breakers should have been handed over to be tried by a judge and jury. Magistrates often had no legal training and local judges were elected and so were often influenced by politics. It was difficult to get juries to convict a man who had killed somebody in a 'fair' fight, and sometimes they were afraid to condemn a gang member for fear of revenge. Federal judges were more effective because they did not depend on local support. One of the most famous in the West was Isaac Parker who for twenty years was judge for West Arkansas and Indian Territory, a district which had been a refuge for lawbreakers of all kinds. At Fort Smith, he appointed 200 deputy marshals with open warrants which gave them a free hand to hunt down any wanted man and a reward if they captured him. During his first few months, he tried ninety-one cases, including eighteen murder cases, of whom fifteen were convicted and eight hanged, six of them all together in public. Parker was criticised for this and for the violent lectures he gave to the convicted criminals and the strong advice he gave the juries. Parker was judge here for twenty years. His friends called him a firm, fair judge, and his critics a bloodthirsty tyrant. But he did make this area of 72,000 square miles less of a refuge for criminals.

The courts spent much of their time dealing with petty crimes but there were more serious cases of murder, robbery, and rioting. These often came from *feuds* between families or between rivals in business. The feud between the Suttons and the Taylors in Texas lasted for fifteen years and involved many members of the family. A feud might begin with a quarrel about money or a woman and when one member of a family was killed, his 'kin' felt they must avenge his death. Disputes arose between cattlemen and sheepmen because the ranchers said that the 'woollies' ate all the grass off the ranges. Ranchers like Charles Goodnight, who did not want trouble, agreed to divide the range with the sheepmen but some cattlemen drove off and killed the sheep by 'rim-rocking' them, that is driving them off the edge of a cliff. Rival groups of cattlemen and traders sometimes clashed, as in the Lincoln County War, west of the Pecos, in which Billy the Kid was involved, and sometimes it was rivalry between ranchers and homesteaders that caused the trouble.

One of the last of these was the Johnson County War in Wyoming in 1892. The members of the Wyoming Stock Growers Association, especially the big cattle companies, had become very annoyed by the farmers' activities. Some of these new settlers certainly were killing or rustling cattle from the big herds, not only when the cattle wandered on to their lands but at other times too. The cattlemen thought most of the homesteaders were thieves. In the town of Buffalo, the centre of Johnson County, the sheriff and townsmen sympathised with the farmers. But the Governor and legislature of the state were on the side of the cattlemen.

Two suspected thieves, one of them a woman, were lynched at the beginning of this 'war'. Then the cattlemen hired a number of Texas cowboys and gunmen in Denver, Colorado, and brought them in a sealed train to Wyoming. Some of the cattlemen were with them when they attacked the farm of a supposed rustler. They shot one man as he came out of the door and besieged the other in the house. Then they set fire to the house and shot the man down as he ran out. A settler saw this and raced to Buffalo to give the alarm. This roused the Buffalo citizens and a crowd of them with the sheriff set out to attack the 73 cattlemen's private army, which took refuge in a ranch house. There the citizens were planning to blow the house up with a wagon-load of explosives when the cavalry arrived. The Governor had at last taken action when he saw the cattlemen in danger and ordered out the troops. The soldiers arrested the cattlemen and the hired gunmen and took them to Cheyenne. Their trial was delayed because Johnson County could not afford to hold it and the court would find it hard to find a jury there who would be fair to the prisoners. Two witnesses to what had happened were arrested for stealing and sent out of the state and did not return. The arrested men were kept in easy imprisonment and then released on bail. The hired gunmen did not turn up for trial and the case against the cattlemen was dismissed.

It is very difficult to find out the truth of this fight. To men like John Clay who was on the cattlemen's side they were a 'gallant band', fighting to defend their rights against a pack of thieves. To men like Mercer, the editor of a Cheyenne paper, they were the 'banditti' of the plains, a lawless mob attacking peaceful farmers. Mercer lost his job for publishing this. On the other hand Johnson County became too hot to hold some of the cattlemen, and they left.

This story shows how the local government officers took sides and how professional gunmen were used. These gunmen were not very like the heroic ones in the stories. They preferred to shoot people from behind cover and from the back rather than face to face in a duel. They often had violent tempers, mean dispositions, a liking for drink and easy money, and not much talent for anything but shooting. Most of them had so many untrue stories told about them, even in their own lifetimes, that it is very difficult to find out exactly what they were like or what they did. Versions of the story of Billy the Kid were nearly as many as the twenty-one men he is supposed to have killed. Teddy Abbott who claimed he worked for John Chisum, a rancher involved in the Lincoln County War but got out *muy pronto* when the war began, said: 'Cowpunchers as a class never had any use for Billy the Kid–it was the Mexicans that made a

Billy the Kid

hero out of him.' The only photograph of him showed him as a rather undersized young man with slightly projecting teeth.

He was said to have been born in New York in 1859 and taken to Kansas when he was three years old. His real name was William Henry Bonney. His father died in Kansas, his mother married again and moved to Silver City in New Mexico where he was supposed to have killed a man who insulted his mother. A song about him said:

> When Billy the Kid was a very young lad,
> In old Silver City he went to the bad,
> Way out in the West with a gun in his hand
> At the age of twelve years he killed his first man.

According to the legend this was the first of twenty-one.

> Fair Mexican maidens play guitars and sing
> A song about Billy their boy bandit king,
> How ere his young manhood had reached its sad end,
> He'd a notch in his pistol for twenty-one men.

In fact he was jailed in Silver City for theft and later killed a blacksmith in Camp Grant, Arizona. The story of his mother was added later and so were the twenty-one men, though he did kill four men and was in gangs that killed others.

He became a cowboy and in 1877 was working for John Tunstall, an Englishman who had a ranch in Lincoln County. Tunstall had set up in business as a trader with a man called McSween, and they were business rivals of another trader, Murphy, Tunstall was determined to get half of every dollar made in Lincoln County and Murphy was determined to stop him. Tunstall was murdered by Murphy's men and the story goes that the Kid swore revenge on the murderers. He certainly went on working for McSween and there was a good deal of fighting between the factions, ending in a battle round McSween's store in Lincoln when McSween and others were killed and the store set on fire. Billy escaped and later became a cattle rustler and horse thief with a gang under him. He was caught by Pat Garrett, the sheriff of Lincoln County, and

REWARD

($5,000.00)

Reward for the capture, dead or alive, of one Wm. Wright, better known as

"BILLY THE KID"

Age, 18. Height, 5 feet, 3 inches. Weight, 125 lbs. Light hair, blue eyes and even features. He is the leader of the worst band of desperadoes the Territory has ever had to deal with. The above reward will be paid for his capture or positive proof of his death.

JIM DALTON, Sheriff.

DEAD OR ALIVE!
"BILLY THE KID"

Reward poster

sentenced to death but escaped after killing two jailers. He was later trapped by Garrett in a Mexican friend's house and shot dead.

> Now this is how Billy the Kid met his fate,
> The bright moon was shining, the hour was late,
> Shot down by Pat Garrett who once was his friend,
> The young outlaw's life had now come to its end.

The Kid was a cattle and horse thief, very serious crimes in cattle country. Other thieves, like Jesse James, specialised in robbing banks and trains. Jesse James had been in the border fighting in Missouri and so had many of the James-Younger

Pat Garrett

Jesse James

gang, who took to robbery instead of going back to civilian life. The gang lasted longer than most. They robbed their first bank in Liberty, Missouri in 1866 and Jesse himself was not killed till 1882. During that time, Frank and Jesse James, Cole and Jim Younger and other members of the gang were hunted by regular sheriffs and marshals and by the Pinkerton Detective Agency employed by the banks. There was some sympathy for these outlaws in Missouri among former Confederate soldiers, especially after James's mother lost her arm, his step-brother was killed and his step-father injured, when some Pinkerton detectives tossed through the window of the house what they claimed was a lighted oil-pot and their critics claimed was a grenade. Jessie and Frank James were not in the house at the time. But the sympathy soon went as the gang killed more and more men in their robberies, cashiers, railroad men or innocent citizens who got in their way.

The gang was blamed for many robberies which they never committed but they did rob many trains and banks. One method of robbing a train was to go to a very small station or halt, force the railroad agent there to put the signals to stop and then hold up the staff of the train to get any valuables being carried, rob the passengers and then ride off. Sometimes they tore up a few yards of track and derailed the train. They did not always make a big profit. In their first train robbery in Iowa when the engine-driver was killed, they obtained only $3,000   79 which, as there were five of them and they risked being hanged if caught, was not very much.

Most of the gang were captured or killed ten years after they started their career when, in 1876, they tried to rob a bank in Northfield, Minnesota, a farming district unused to the outlaws of the south and west. But the citizens proved more warlike than they expected. Several fired on the gang. Two of the bandits were killed, and the three Younger brothers and Frank James were wounded. The Younger brothers were caught and imprisoned for life but the James brothers escaped. They returned to crime with a second-rate gang, one of whom made a deal with the law and shot Jesse James in the back. Frank James gave himself up and was acquitted and lived till 1916. He and Cole Younger who had been released, owing to the efforts of a man whose life he had saved in the war, were two of the very few members of the gang to die a natural death. Most of them were shot, lynched or committed suicide. Even in the lawless west crime did not always pay.

There's many a man with a face fine and fair,
Who starts out in life with chance to be square,
But just like poor Billy he wanders astray
And loses his life in the very same way.

The west was certainly not a peaceful place in these years but the majority of the people were not outlaws and bandits; many of them did not even carry one gun, let alone two, and the people who moved in were anxious to establish lawful government as soon as possible. The time when people made their own law did not last long; in Abilene it was only five years after the arrival of the first herds that the town government asked the cattlemen not to come to the town. Schools, churches, newspapers, shops followed the first buildings very quickly and the wild west became much tamer.

8 The Fate of the Indians

The end of the buffalo. 40,000 died to provide the pile of hides at Dodge City in about 1874

The coming of the railroads, the cattlemen and the farmers meant the end of the Indians' way of life. It had begun to change long before, when white traders brought them guns, cloth, alcohol and white men's diseases, but the killing of the buffalo brought the biggest change. The huge herds of millions of buffalo which had roamed the prairies, had provided the Indians with their food, clothing, *lodges*, tools, weapons and fuel. Between 1860 and 1880 these herds were nearly wiped out by hunters who shot them for their hides, not for the meat, which they left rotting on the ground. Teddy Abbott thought this was done on purpose:

> All this slaughter was a put-up job on the part of the government to control the Indians by getting rid of their food supply and it was a low-down dirty way of doing the business.

Even if it was not deliberate, the killing of the buffalo drove the Indians to the *reservations*.

But the Plains Indians did not accept this without a fight. They were war-like tribes who thought hunting and fighting were the only work worthy of a man. Comanches, Arapahoes, Cheyennes, Sioux, Nez Perces and Apaches all attacked the settlers and fought the army. It would take too long to tell the whole story, so we shall look at two tribes who were among those who fought longest and hardest, the Sioux and Cheyennes.

The Sioux were divided into different groups who did not always agree with each other but would sometimes unite against the whites. The Cheyennes had been divided earlier into the northern and southern branches and the Northern Cheyenne had intermarried with the Sioux and sometimes fought on their side. They ranged the country from present-day Minnesota through the Dakotas to Wyoming and Montana, but were gradually being pushed west. Because they lived by hunting, they needed hundreds of square miles of land through which they moved with their *tepees* and goods loaded on *travois* drawn by horses and dogs. White people had crossed this area from the time that Lewis and Clark had explored it in 1804–5. They were sometimes attacked by Indians but it was in the 1860s, when miners moved into Colorado and Montana and the cattlemen moved further west, that the Cheyennes and Sioux fought most fiercely, though it was then too late to save their hunting grounds. They had been slow to believe that the treaty of 1851 which guaranteed their land would be broken, but the prospect of gold or good land or a change of government in Washington often meant the end of treaties. Later an old Indian said: 'They made us many promises, more than I can remember, but they never kept but one; they promised to take our land and they took it.'

The miners in the Colorado wanted the Indians out, so the Cheyennes under Black Kettle were ordered to a new reservation in Sand Creek. At first they would not go and went on attacking the whites but in 1864, about 500 of them moved there and camped peacefully. They thought that an officer of the U.S. army had guaranteed a truce. At Sand Creek they were attacked by about 1,000 Colorado militia under Colonel Chivington who encouraged them to kill all the Indians. There was an official enquiry later and one officer said:

> There seemed to be no organisation among our troops, every one on his own hook, shots flying between our ranks. White Antelope ran towards our columns unarmed and with both arms raised but was killed.

The officer tried to tell Chivington that the Indians were there under a flag of truce.

> His reply was, bringing his fist close down to my face, 'Damn any man who sympathised with Indians. . . .' He had come to kill Indians and believed it to be honorable to kill Indians under any and all circumstances.

But many Americans disagreed with Chivington and were horrified at the massacre. The Cheyennes naturally found it difficult to trust the white man's word after this and were the more ready to continue to kill settlers and burn and steal their property.

Black Kettle was killed in 1865 at the battle of the Washita where Colonel Custer and his men surrounded a Cheyenne village on a winter's night. The Indians did not expect the soldiers to go on fighting in the bitter winter cold and were taken by surprise. About a hundred warriors and thirty-eight women and children were killed. After this the Cheyennes moved north to fight with the Sioux against the whites.

The Sioux had several strong chiefs at this time and in 1866 Crazy Horse and Red Cloud led them against the soldiers who were guarding a new road from Fort Laramie to the mining towns of Montana. This road ran through a favourite Sioux hunting ground where there were hills, trees and good game. Red Cloud later became a friend of James Cook, and told him that

> he well knew that it was then or never that the white man 83

Sitting Bull; a Sioux leader

Red Cloud; a Sioux chief   *General Custer*

could be stayed from doing as he pleased with the valuable hunting grounds which the Chief had so long contested with the Crows.

A detachment of eighty soldiers was wiped out by Red Cloud's men.

But Red Cloud only delayed the white men. He did not stop them. A new treaty was made in 1868 and the Sioux agreed to go to a reservation, if the army abandoned the road to Montana. The government plan was to concentrate the Indians in two big reservations, one in the Black Hills of Dakota and one in Indian Territory in present-day Oklahoma. Red Cloud and some Sioux chiefs agreed to go on the reservation but some, including Crazy Horse and Sitting Bull, would not. This treaty might have lasted a little longer than it did if Custer had not taken an expedition to the Black Hills, which were sacred ground to the Indians, to see if gold could be found there. Unfortunately for the Sioux, it was, and gold hungry prospectors poured in to land which was supposed to belong to the Sioux. More and more Sioux went off to join Crazy Horse and Sitting Bull and the other chiefs who would not accept any treaty with the whites. Red Cloud stayed on the reservation at the Pine Ridge *agency*, and this lost him the admiration of the younger warriors.

The army was called in to force the Indians on to the reservations. Under General Terry, they advanced against the Sioux in the area of the Rosebud river. One Cheyenne village was destroyed but the soldiers had to retreat. General Crook met Crazy Horse at the battle of the Rosebud in which both sides lost some men and withdrew. The other half of the force advanced up the Rosebud and Custer's Seventh cavalry were sent ahead to find out where the main Indian force was and report back. Custer's orders were a little vague and he took it to mean that he could attack. When he found a very large village on the Little Bighorn river, he did attack. The Indians drove back one section of the force at first, but Custer had circled round to attack from another position. He was outnumbered but must have decided to fight all the same, after sending a message to the other companies asking them to come to his support. Nobody knows exactly what he did decide because he and all his men were killed in the battle. The only living sign of the Seventh Cavalry left was Comanche, a horse belonging to one of the officers. The companies left behind heard the firing but they themselves were being attacked and did not go to Custer's help.

This was the Indians' biggest victory but, though they had won the battle, they had lost the war. Custer became a national hero and the Americans were more determined than ever to defeat the Sioux. The army pursued and fought the different groups one by one. Led by Sitting Bull, some escaped to Canada. Crazy Horse surrendered in 1877 and was taken to the Red Cloud Agency, but he was still defiant and unrepentant. He was arrested because of this and was killed while trying to fight his way out.

Some of the Cheyennes had fought with the Sioux, so they were all sent south to Indian territory, not to the Sioux reservation where they had hoped to go. They hated this. This hot, dry, bare, flat country was very different from the cool mountains, the pine trees and the clear streams of their northern lands. Many of their people died of *consumption* and *dysentery*. They wanted to go home. The soldiers had promised that they should go home if they did not like it, but the promise was not kept.

In September 1878, led by Dull Knife and Little Wolf, nearly 300 of them including eighty-seven men and boys old enough to fight, left their lodges standing and their fires burning and stole out of the reservation. They managed to catch some horses and when morning came and their escape was discovered, they were far away. The soldiers followed. Little Wolf tried to talk to them to explain that they were only going back home but the soldiers attacked. The Indian guns frightened the soldiers' horses and the Cheyennes lit prairie fires which made the soldiers withdraw.

The Cheyennes moved on through Kansas, killing cattle, stealing horses and killing some settlers. The chiefs did not want 86 people killed but they could not always stop their young men.

Dull Knife (seated) with Little Wolf; Cheyenne chiefs

Sometimes when the Cheyennes camped, they had songs and dances to hearten them. With them was Little Finger Nail, a singer and artist, who drew pictures of what happened in a big book which he always kept with him. Twice more the soldiers attacked but the Cheyennes drove them off and slipped away quietly, moving fast through country they knew well. They crossed many rivers and creeks and three railway lines. Then just north of the Union Pacific line, 600 miles away from the reservation, Dull Knife and Little Wolf decided to separate. Dull Knife wanted to go to the Sioux reservation where he hoped Red Cloud would shelter his people, but Little Wolf wanted to go right on to the Yellowstone river.

Dull Knife reached the Sioux but Red Cloud's agency was surrounded by soldiers and he could not help the Cheyennes. Dull Knife and his people were captured and taken to Fort Robinson. There he was told that they must go back to Indian

Territory. Dull Knife refused. 'I am here on my own ground; I will never go back.' They were kept in the barracks. Their guns were taken away but the soldiers did not get them all because the Indians took them apart and hid the pieces. At first they were treated kindly but the army had orders to make them go back. In January 1879, when the temperature was $-18°C$, the commander cut off first their food, then their fuel and then their water to force them to go back. Two of their leaders went to speak to the officer but were put in chains. The doors of their wooden prison were barred more securely and many were afraid that the soldiers planned to burn them all to death. So, one night, 130 people in the barracks broke out and made for the rough land beyond the river. Half of the men were killed before they reached it and groups of others were hunted down. A group of thirty-four, among them Little Finger Nail, made a last stand against the soldiers in a hole in the prairie. Only seven women and children were left alive at the end of the fight. Little Finger Nail's picture book was strapped to his back still but there were two bullet holes through it. Altogether at the end, seventy-eight were left alive, including Dull Knife. Most of them were at last sent to the Sioux agency but the Kansas settlers insisted on some of them being tried for murder because they had killed white settlers. Some were sent but released at the trial for lack of evidence. By this time many white people felt some sympathy with the Cheyennes and even admiration for their 1,000 mile journey back to their home land.

Meanwhile, Little Wolf had camped for the winter in Lost Chokecherry valley and his scouts kept in touch with what was going on. The soldiers never found him and in the spring he continued his journey to the Yellowstone river and surrendered to an army lieutenant whom he trusted. This time they were not sent south but given a reservation on the Tongue river but, like the Sioux, they disliked reservation life.

The Sioux were on one big reservation north of Nebraska but the different groups were settled in different parts of it, so there were six Indian agents in charge of it. The *Indian Bureau* in Washington decided that the Indians should be taught to

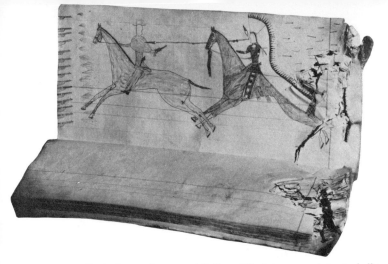

Little Finger Nail's book; cavalryman and Indians. The hole was made by the bullet which killed him

farm and educated to follow the white man's road. Sitting Bull and the others who had gone to Canada did not give themselves up until 1881. This group would not accept the agents' attempts to turn them into farmers and send their children to school. Even Red Cloud and the others who had not joined in the war were reluctant to part with their children. Farming they considered beneath them and they thought white men owed them a living because they had taken away their land and buffalo. They could not see any advantage in taking the white man's road, especially as many of the white farmers in that area were very poor because of the poor soil and summer droughts. The agents tried to break the power of the chiefs and the tribal council by dealing with the Indians as individuals. The army used Indians as scouts to track other Indians and the agents formed an Indian police force to keep order. These police were usually loyal to the agent as their new chief but they were often unwilling to arrest their fellow tribesmen.

Some agents were better than others at getting on with their charges. The reservations were fairly peaceful as long as the agents did not try to push farming and education too forcefully and as long as the food rations arrived promptly. But in 1890 the Sioux were in a discontented mood. A new agreement had

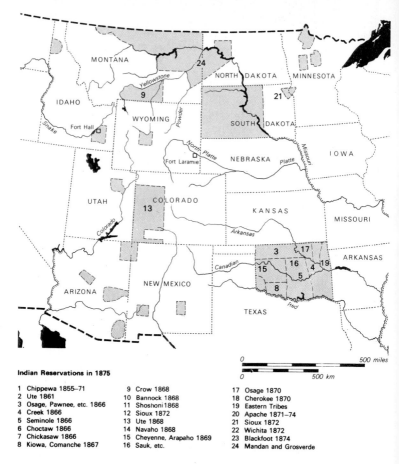

Indian Reservations in 1875

1 Chippewa 1855–71	9 Crow 1868	17 Osage 1870
2 Ute 1861	10 Bannock 1868	18 Cherokee 1870
3 Osage, Pawnee, etc. 1866	11 Shoshoni 1868	19 Eastern Tribes
4 Creek 1866	12 Sioux 1872	20 Apache 1871–74
5 Seminole 1866	13 Ute 1868	21 Sioux 1872
6 Choctaw 1866	14 Navaho 1868	22 Wichita 1872
7 Chickasaw 1866	15 Cheyenne, Arapaho 1869	23 Blackfoot 1874
8 Kiowa, Comanche 1867	16 Sauk, etc.	24 Mandan and Grosverde

been made with them in 1889. The government had decided to try to settle the Indians on homesteads like white people, and the Sioux were persuaded to give up nine million acres of their reservation for white settlement on the understanding that they should be allowed either to own land or to remain protected. Other promises were made but not kept. The years from 1887 to 1890 were years of drought and then the government cut the beef ration. The Sioux were hungry and many of their children were dying.

90   At this moment news reached the Sioux that there was a

prophet or Messiah beyond the western mountains who preached that the Indians could win back their way of life. Some of the chief men were sent to ask about this. Among them were Kicking Bear and Short Bull. The Messiah was a *Piute* Indian, Wovoka, the orphaned son of a medicine man. He had been brought up as a Christian by a white family. Wovoka had a vision during an eclipse of the sun. If the Indians were honest, hard-working and peaceful and danced the Ghost Dance, a new land would arise in the sky and push the white people back across the ocean to the east, all the dead Indians would return to earth and, best of all, the buffalo would come back and they would all go back to their own way of life. This would all happen in the spring of 1891.

The Ghost Dance was danced after a *sweat-bath* and a time of fasting. The people formed a circle and moved very quickly round and round. Some fell in a trance and, if they did, they would go for a short visit to their dead friends and hear about the new world coming. They must wear a canvas or cotton shirt covered with special signs. This message spread through all the western tribes but led to fighting only among the Sioux. Kicking Bear and Short Bull brought the news back with some alterations. They said that a dust-storm would arise and sweep all the white men away and that the ghost shirt was bullet-proof. This was not so peaceful as Wovoka's message but the Ghost Dance might not have caused trouble but for the reduced rations and the broken promises. Some of the agents had little trouble with the dancers and were in favour of letting it die out but a new agent sent to Pine Ridge, called by the Indians Young-man-afraid-of-his-Sioux, became worried and asked for troops to be sent. James Cook was a scout at Pine Ridge during the Ghost Dance 'war'. He reckoned that if the Sioux were allowed to dance, they would soon wear themselves out and become tired of it.

Not all the chiefs supported it. American Horse and Young-man-afraid-of-his-horses would have nothing to do with it. Red Cloud, old and nearly blind, would not support it, nor would Gall, who had led the attack at the battle of the Little Bighorn.

But many, like Big Foot and Hump, joined Kicking Bear and stirred up the young men to join. Some of the most eager were those who had been sent east to white schools. Some chiefs wanted to be sure either way. As one said:

My friends, if this is a good thing, we shall have it; if it is not possible it will fall to the earth itself. So you had better learn to dance, so if the Messiah does come he will not pass us by, but will help us to get back our hunting grounds and buffalo.

The man with the biggest reputation among the Sioux, Sitting Bull, did not believe altogether in the Ghost Dance but he did not oppose it and he let it be danced in his village. General Miles, who was in charge of the troops sent to the reservation, wanted him arrested but the agent would not act until he was given government orders. Then he sent an Indian police force to arrest him. At first he went peacefully but then began to struggle. His friends rushed forward to help. One wounded a police sergeant who then shot Sitting Bull. In the struggle that followed Sitting Bull, one of his sons, six policemen and several others were killed or wounded.

This made the Sioux angry and frightened and many scattered to different parts of the reservation. General Miles worked hard to persuade them to return to the agency and he was having some success when they were scattered again after the battle of Wounded Knee.

At Wounded Knee creek about four or five hundred Sioux, under Big Foot, were coming slowly towards the reservation. Soldiers of the Seventh Cavalry, Custer's old regiment, caught up with them, and their commander insisted that the Indians should give up their weapons. The men had to sit in the snow in a semicircle while some were sent to bring in the guns. Big Foot had pneumonia but he came to sit with the others. The search produced only two old guns. The officer knew there were more and sent scouts and soldiers to search. One of the medicine men tried to stir up the men against the soldiers. Some of the
92 young men took guns from under their blankets and fired at the

soldiers who fired back. This started a general battle. Little Bat, a half-breed scout and a friend of James Cook told him about it. He had been one of those searching the tents when the firing broke out:

In a moment death reigned on all sides. The *Hotchkiss* guns, trained on the Indian lodges, opened fire, and the Indian women and children who but a few minutes before had been told they were in no danger, were killed and wounded by the score. Some of the soldiers who were with Little Bat among the lodges were killed. Bat had taken no fire-arms with him when he went to the lodges with the troopers, for he wanted to impress the Indians with the conviction that they were in no danger. His clothing was pierced by bullets as he tried to get to his own tent, where his weapons had been left. When I met Little Bat soon after the affair, he

Wounded Knee; the frozen body of Big Foot after the 'battle'

told me that the sights he had witnessed during that killing of women and children would never be effaced from his memory.

Miles was very angry with the officer in command because the massacre made things worse. He surrounded the reservation with troops and gradually edged the Sioux back in towards the centre of the reservation with no further battles. The faith of the Sioux in the ghost dance had been shaken because many of the Indians killed at Wounded Knee had been wearing the Ghost Shirt. Gradually they all gave in and none was punished except a group of about twenty who were sent to Europe with Buffalo Bill's Wild West show, an undignified but fairly mild penalty.

This was the last war of the Sioux against the white men, in fact the last Indian war, because by then even the fierce Apaches under Geronimo had surrendered, though in the end it took 5,000 soldiers to make them. The old leaders died and some of the younger ones took up cattle ranching or farming. Some left the reservation to become citizens and some stayed, but their old way of life was gone for ever.

Teddy Abbott sympathised with them. He talked to a Sioux:

> We got to the subject of the old days. I said: 'You fellows used to have a pretty good time.'
>
> He said: 'Yes', and then he described the way they used to live before the white men came. They would go down to a creek and camp where there was good water and grass, run a bunch of buffalo down and skin them and get the meat—then when the grass got a little short, they would just move on to a place where there was new grass and keep that up, no trouble or worries and when one wife got old, they'd marry another one.
>
> Coming back up Dog Creek, I met *Russell*. I said: 'God, I wish I'd been a Sioux Indian a hundred years ago,' and I told him the story.
>
> He said: 'Ted, there's a pair of us. They've been living in heaven for a thousand years and we took it away from them for forty dollars a month.'

9 The End of the Open Range

It was not only the Indians' way of life that was changing in the 1890s, but also the cattlemen's. Charles Goodnight once said that 'if all the good luck and all the bad luck I've had were put together, I reckon it'd make the biggest damned pile of luck in the world'. The 'seventies and early 'eighties had been the years of good luck. Prices were high and more and more cattle were brought on to the ranges, so that they were over-stocked even in good years, and drought or blizzards could be disastrous. The bad luck came in 1885-7. In 1885 there was a bad winter on the southern ranges of Kansas, Colorado and the Panhandle, and many cattle died. In the summer of 1886 there was a drought and the grass was poor. Then in 1886 came the worst winter anybody remembered on the ranges of Montana and Wyoming. In the fall many people noticed that the beaver were working day and night, storing twice as much food as usual. The animals had thicker fur and the ducks and geese went south a month early. The haze was high in the Indian summer and there were haloes round the sun. All these were thought to be signs of a bad winter to come. There was no wet snow storm as usual, but in November there was a heavy blizzard of hard, dry snow. The *chinook* came as usual in January but it was followed by a two-day blizzard, the worst ever known, and then the cold and snow continued without relief.

Granville Stuart sold some of his cattle and sent Abbott with another herd across the Missouri to the foot of the Rockies. He and a fellow cowboy rode out in the bitter cold to try to save some at least of the stock. The temperature sometimes dropped to —48°C. In England we think it very cold indeed if it is —5°C. Abbott dressed to suit the weather.

> I wore two pairs of wool socks, a pair of moccasins, a pair of Dutch socks that came up to the knees, a pair of government overshoes, two suits of heavy underwear, pants, overalls, chaps and a big heavy shirt. I got a pair of women's stockings and cut the feet out and made sleeves. I wore wool gloves and great big heavy mittens, a blanket-lined sourdough overcoat and a great big sealskin cap.

Even then he was not too warm.

All Granville's efforts to save his stock were not successful. He lost sixty-six per cent of his herds. In 1886 he had 40,000 and in 1887 there were about 7,000. In 1886 they had branded 10,000 of his calves. In 1887 there were just a hundred at the spring round-up. The dry cows and the older tough steers were the ones that survived. Even so Stuart did better than many of the ranchers, especially the big cattle companies. His cattle were nearly all northern range-bred cattle. Many of the others came from the states farther east or had been cross-bred with less hardy animals. There were too many of them on the ranges; they drifted before the northern storms trying to find better weather or food but there was none. When they came to a drift fence, they lay down and died and the bodies of thousands were found piled there in the spring. The people of Great Falls, Missouri, saw the thin starving cattle looming out of the snow, part of a herd of 5,000 which had moved south.

Stuart was sickened by the deaths. 'I wanted no more of it. I never wanted to own again an animal that I could not feed or shelter.' Many ranchers had no choice in the matter. Their losses made them bankrupt. This was specially so of the ranchers from the east and the cattle companies. Medora, the centre of the ranges where Roosevelt had lived, became a ghost town. The population was 'eleven including the chickens when they're all in town'. Even the big companies like the Swan Cattle company and the Powder Valley company, financed by investors in England, lost all their money. They had borrowed

at high rates of interest to stock the ranches and the losses of

The last of the 5,000. Charles Russell's drawing of the wolves waiting for a lean, starved steer to die in the great blizzard

cattle ruined them. The western-bred ranchers did better, especially the small cattlemen, who owned only one or two thousand cattle and were able to provide food for at least some of them in the winter.

These bad years came at a time when there were other changes in the cattle industry. The open unfenced range was coming to an end. Drift fences had been built in quite early days but by 1885 many farmers and some cattlemen were beginning to fence land. This had been difficult earlier on because wooden fences were expensive in the treeless plains and hedges took a long time to grow. But in 1874 a new kind of wire came on the market, barbed wire. Some cattlemen, especially those who did not want the land fenced, thought this was barbarous. Before they got used to it, horses and cattle were injured running against it, but when they stopped doing this, it proved to be far the best way of keeping them in or of keeping other people's out. 97

A sod house in Nebraska; some of the people have dressed up for the photograph, some are in working clothes

This was what the ranchers objected to, because homesteaders fenced in their farm land and the cattle did not have so much land to wander over. In some areas men, sometimes masked, went out to cut the wire but this did not last long, as the more far-sighted ranchers saw that it had come to stay.

The homesteaders and cattlemen, as we have seen in the Johnson County war, were not often good friends. The farmers used less land and grew mixed crops on it. Some of the settlers in the north-west were new immigrants, Germans and Scandinavians, who were poor and unused to American ways, but native American farmers were more ready to assert their rights and fight if the cowboys cut their fences and shut them out from streams and water-holes. By law they were in the right, but it was difficult for a farmer to appeal to the federal laws when most of the state legislature, the governor, the sheriffs and the judges were connected with the big cattlemen. The farmers had the bigger numbers and at election time they could and sometimes did out-vote the ranchers.

So, for all the ranchers' opposition, the farmers' frontier moved west and the cattlemen found that, if they were to survive at all, they had to use some of the farmers' methods. They, too, began to use fences and after their experience in 1886, more of them started to grow hay, *alfalfa* and other crops to feed their stock in winter, as Charles Goodnight had done for years. They found that they could do better in the drier parts of the country than the farmers, especially when the windmills were introduced to pump water from the wells for irrigation and water supply. The strong dry prairie winds which the farmers' wives hated, now provided power for the windmills. A farmer who took only a section of land in this part of the west found things difficult because it was far too big to irrigate it for crops and too small for cattle. So the cattlemen could still make a living from Texas to Montana along this belt of arid land and still do.

10 The Legend of the West

We have already seen how legends grew up round characters
like Billy the Kid. The whole story of the last frontier has
become part of the folk-history of the United States. In fact it
became a legend while it was still in existence, although, as one
old cowboy put it: 'The average old-time range-man would
not have known a folk-tale from Adam's off ox.' Many cowboys
lived long enough to read the stories and see the films about
their life and times. They were very ready to pick out mistakes.
Teddy Abbott had something to say about them:

> That Emerson Hough movie 'North of '36' was supposed to
> show one of the early cattle drives to the railroad. It was
> pretty good, except that the moving picture people had
> Taisie Lockheed [the heroine] coming up the trail wearing
> pants. If the cowpunchers of them days had ever seen a
> woman wearing pants, they'd have stampeded to the brush.

Stories about Wild Bill Hickok and Billy the Kid were published in their lifetime in cheap dime editions and in magazines.
Novels about the west soon appeared. One or two of the early
writers had been cowboys themselves but one of the most
famous novels, 'The Virginian', was written by Owen Wister, a
novelist. It had many of the characters and situations that
appeared in later stories, including the quarrel over the
gambling table. Trampas, the villain of the story, has just made
his bet:

> It was now the Virginian's turn to bet or leave the game and
> he did not speak at once.

DETECTIVE LIBRARY

JESSE JAMES

FRANK JAMES

THE ONLY LIBRARY CONTAINING TRUE STORIES OF THE JAMES BOYS.

Entered according to Act of Congress, in the year 1897, by FRANK TOUSEY, in the Office of the Librarian of Congress, Washington, D. C. Entered at the Post Office, at New York, N. Y., as Second Class Matter. The subscription price of Detective Library by the year is $2.50; $1.25 per six months, post-paid.

No. 750. | COMPLETE. | FRANK TOUSEY, PUBLISHER, 34 & 36 NORTH MOORE STREET, N. Y. | PRICE | Vol. I.
New York, April 9, 1897. | ISSUED EVERY FRIDAY. | 10 CENTS.

THE JAMES BOYS;
AND THE FORTY NINERS.
BY D. W. STEVENS.

NED JACKSON

Cover of a ten cent novel published in 1897

Therefore Trampas spoke, 'Your bet, you son-of-a———.'

The Virginian's pistol came out and his hand lay on the table, holding it unaimed. And with a voice as gentle as ever . . . but drawling a little more than usual so that there was almost a space between each word, he issued his orders to the man Trampas:

'When you call me that, smile.' And he looked at Trampas across the table.

Trampas did not draw his gun until the end of the book when the Virginian shot him dead.

This was the first of thousands of cowboy novels. The first of many films was made in 1903. Some actors like Tom Mix had actually been cowboys but the films became less and less like real life. James Cook or Teddy Abbott would find it very difficult to recognise themselves in the gun-slinging cowboys of the films, just as Crazy Horse and Little Wolf would find it difficult to see themselves either as blood-thirsty savages or noble red men.

Billy the Kid would not recognise himself at all. When he was killed, there was relief in New Mexico that this thief and murderer was dead. In legend he became a kind of American Robin Hood. The few facts known about him were altered or embroidered to suit the new version. The insult to his mother was added to justify his first murder. The jailers he killed, reported as well-liked local men in the newspapers at the time, became wicked villains who tortured poor Billy. Pat Garrett became the treacherous friend who shot Billy without warning. In view of the Kid's record this was the only way to shoot him, and stay alive! Many of the stories are invented and show him as much better or much worse than he was. As in the Robin Hood stories it is the outlaw who becomes the hero.

In the many pictures of 'Custer's Last Stand' Custer is shown as an heroic figure surrounded by his men, all dead but him. In fact nobody knows whether he died first or last. The Indians did not say and there were no survivors to tell the story. Many

people claimed to be sole survivors and told the story of Custer's

Film cowboys. John Wayne in 'Red River' prepares to punish the cook who started a stampede. He was stealing sugar and knocked down some pans which started the herd running

Last Stand. In the end there were more sole survivors than there were men in the battle! One story was that a Sioux, Rain-in-the-face, killed Custer and cut his heart out. Longfellow wrote a poem telling the story.

> But the foemen fled in the night
> And Rain-in-the-face in his flight
> Uplifted high in the air,
> As a ghastly trophy bore
> The brave heart that beat no more,
> Of White Chief with Yellow Hair.

In fact Custer's body was the only one not mutilated by the Indians. Nobody knows who did kill Custer. The Sioux could not say and the Cheyennes did not even know he was there. But

One of the many imaginary pictures of Custer's last stand. Still on his feet, he fires with both guns

pictures of Custer's Last Stand were painted and one of them was distributed by a brewing company as an advertisement, so it appeared in a lot of bars. Custer had been involved in politics and it suited some people to make a hero of him and his wife was determined that he should be remembered as a brave man even if she had to invent evidence to prove it.

Most of the legends have been about the cowboy and Indian period of the frontier. Perhaps it was because there were more people in the east to write and talk about it, and railroads and telegraphs to carry the news. Perhaps it was the horses that seemed to make cowboys and Indians larger than life. To the cowboy, herding cattle was just a job. Sometimes he liked it, sometimes he disliked it and he often grumbled about the pay. It is still a job for some. One of them working on a Wyoming ranch was interviewed on a television programme in 1962:

> Doug Douglas, a twenty-three year old cowboy on this ranch, who began working at fifteen at a salary of $90 a month plus room and board, is now earning $150. He spends fourteen hours a day in the saddle, riding approximately forty miles; his excursions to town include drinking beer, watching television, and eating chicken. 'I've seen a lot of sorry Hollywood western movies,' was his comment regarding his impressions of western film fare.

James Cook and Ted Abbott would probably find more in common to talk about to this real cowboy than to the cowboys shown on the films.

Where To Find Out More

BOOKS

ANDY ADAMS	*Trail Drive*, Whiting and Wheaton
F. COLLINSON	*Life in the Saddle*, University of Oklahoma
C. DAVIS	*The North American Indian*, Hamlyn
P. GOBLE and D. GOBLE	*Custer's Last Battle*, Macmillan
ALAN LOMAX, ed.	*The Penguin Book of American Folk-songs*, Penguin Books
B. P. RINNERT	*The Cowboy*, Collier-Macmillan

Books by James Cook and Teddy Abbott are not easy to find but can be obtained through a public library:

JAMES F. COOK	*Fifty Years on the Old Frontier*, University of Oklahoma Press
E. ABBOTT and H. H. SMITH	*We Pointed them North*, University of Oklahoma Press

FILMS

The First Americans and *Cowboys, woollies and sod-busters* (BBC/TV) are about the modern west.

Cheyenne Autumn and *Red River* are two good 'westerns' on this subject.

MUSEUM

The American Museum at Claverton Manor, Bath, has a section on western history.

Things To Do

1 From atlases and picture books, find out more about the country through which the western railroads passed and see what difficulties had to be overcome.
2 As in Britain, many U.S. railroads have been closed down and motorways are used instead. Find out where the big highways run (they are all numbered) and see how their routes compare with the railroads. 'The Times' Atlas of the Americas shows this.
3 Make up a song for modern road builders like those written for the railroad builders.
4 Write a scenario (outline plan) for a western film based on one of the incidents described in the book and act it.
5 Find more of the western songs. Listen to 'Billy the Kid' and 'Rodeo', ballet music composed by Aaron Copland.
6 Using a popular tune, make up a song to go with a type of work, as the cowboys did.
7 Write a front page for a newspaper in a cattle town a week after the first of the cattle herds from Texas came in.
8 Write a list of ten laws for a new cattle or railroad town.
9 Make a book of pictures for the Cheyenne escape from Indian territory, as Little Finger Nail did, or for the Sioux wars.
10 Think of something you want as much as the Sioux wanted the buffalo back and make up a dance for it as they did.
11 This book describes only the Sioux. Find out how the Apaches under Cochise and Geronimo, the Comanches under Quamah Parker and the Nez Perces under Chief Joseph, defended their lands.
12 Debate the arguments for the Indians and the white people in the settlement of the Great Plains.

Glossary

Note: Sp. = Spanish. Many of the Texas cowboys could speak Spanish or used Spanish words learned on the Mexican border.

adobe, sun-dried bricks made of clay (Sp.)

agency, the central buildings of a reservation where the Indian agent had his headquarters

alfalfa, a plant providing good food for grazing

alkaline, full of a soluble salt which makes the water very hard

bandana, a large cotton scarf

bowie knife, a large hunting knife with a handle guard and a blade about ten to fifteen inches long, adapted for use in knife fights; called after Jim Bowie, a frontiersman who died at the battle of the Alamo

brand, mark made with a hot iron on animal's hide to prove ownership

bull-whacker, driver of a wagon drawn by oxen

cañon or *canyon*, deep ravine or gorge, narrow valley between steep cliffs

capper, a man who persuaded people to come into a gambling saloon

carbine, short-barrelled, light-weight rifle

chaparejos, wide leather leg-coverings, called chaps for short (Sp.)

chinook, warm dry wind, blowing down the east side of the Rockies

chuck-wagon, wagon with the chuck or food box on the back (see picture, p. 52)

cocinero, cook (Sp.)

Confederacy, Southern states which joined together before the Civil War to form a separate nation

Confederates, men from the Confederacy

consumption, a disease of the lungs, also known as tuberculosis; many Indians got this when crowded together in reservations instead of living in the open air

corral, fenced enclosure for cattle or horses (Sp.)

coyote, prairie wolf

decoy, something or somebody used to lure people or animals into a trap

to *designate*, to name, mark out

dime, slang word for ten cents or one-tenth of a dollar

Dixie, word used for the Southern states; a song written in 1859, popular with southern soldiers in the Civil War

dogies, motherless calves

drift fence, fence built to stop cattle drifting or moving off the range

dude, very fashionably dressed man: someone from the eastern U.S.A. who did not know western ways

Dutch oven, a heavy pot with a tight-fitting lid which could be put on an open fire or have hot coals put on top of it

dysentery, disease caused by germs in food or water

erosion, wearing away

faro, a gambling game in which bets are placed on a special table

federal, belonging to the central government in Washington; each state also has a separate government

feud, war of revenge between groups or families carried on for a long time; common in the southern states in the nineteenth century

flat-car, railroad wagon consisting of a flat piece of wood on wheels used for carrying rails and timber for railroad building

freight, load of goods on ship, train, wagon, etc.

fusillade, burst of continued shots from firearms

gauge, width between railroad tracks

gauger, man whose job it was to see that the gauge was correct

gradient, slope of hill

gulch, short, steep-sided ravine

half-breed, half Indian, half white

hobbles, short ropes tying together two of a horse's legs to stop it wandering too far

holster, leather case for pistol or rifle

homestead, *Homestead Act*, farm. After the Homestead Act, every householder could have 160 acres of land if he settled on it free

homesteader, farmer on a homestead; sometimes called sod-busters or nesters

Hotchkiss gun, an early type of machine gun which could fire rapidly

Indian Bureau, government department responsible for Indians

Jehu, a king in the Old Testament who drove a chariot very fast

kin, relations

lariat, see *lasso*

latitude, distance north or south of the equator measured as part of an angle of 90°. You will find the lines marked on a map. These lines 109 circling the globe are called parallels

lasso, lariat, long rope with loop for catching horses or cattle (Sp.)

lodge, tent made of canvas or hides spread over poles used by Plains Indians; sometimes called a tepee or tipi

lot, plot of ground

to *lynch,* to kill a man without a trial

maverick, an unbranded calf not following his mother; many people thought these could be taken by anyone but some thought this dishonest

militia, citizens called on to serve as an army in time of danger; they did not have much military training

molasses, thick, dark, sweet syrup

monte, a card game

Mormons, members of the Church of Latter-Day Saints who were pioneers in Utah

muy pronto, very quickly (Sp.)

nitro-glycerine, explosive made by mixing glycerine with sulphuric acid and nitric acid; it had the advantage that it could be made on the spot

option, a right to choose land to take in the future

ordinance, regulation

outfit, a ranch and the men who worked on it

Panhandle, north-west corner of Texas; it sticks out from the main part so that the shape of the state is a little like a pan with a handle

parallel, see *latitude*

Piutes, a tribe of Indians living west of the Rocky mountains

poker, a card game

posse, group of able-bodied men called on by the sheriff to help him catch a criminal

premature, too early

punk, decayed wood, very dry and crumbly, used as tinder

quirt, whip

remuda, herd of horses (Sp.)

Renaissance, period of history in the fifteenth and sixteenth century, famous for great paintings

reservation, land set aside for Indians to live on under government protection

roustabout, common labourer: here means a dishonest one

Russell, Charles Russell, a cowboy, but best-known as an artist

rustler, cattle thief

saleratus, baking soda used to make bread or biscuits rise

110 *section,* here means one square mile, or 640 acres; all unsettled land in

the U.S.A. was surveyed and divided into sections

seven-up, card game

six-bits, one bit = one-eighth of a dollar

sledges, sledge hammer

sod huts, huts or houses built of turf or sods cut from the prairie; used because of the shortage of wood

steer, a young castrated bull

Stetson, broad-brimmed flat hat with high crown; Stetson was the trade-mark

sweat-bath, steam bath in small covered hut to sweat out dirt

tarriers, terriers, Irish railroad labourers

tepees, Indian tents of hide or canvas (see *lodges*)

terminus, *termini*, end place or places, for example of a road or railway

Territories, land on the frontier where there were not enough people to have a State government, so officials were appointed by the government in Washington

Texas Rangers, special police in the state of Texas

topographer, one who makes detailed descriptions, maps, etc. of places

tornado, strong, whirling wind that blows along a narrow path

travois, sledge made of lodge or tent poles to drag goods when Indians move

Uncle Sam's Injuns, Indians living on a reservation. Uncle Sam is a popular expression for the U.S. government

vaquero, cowboy (Sp.)

vigilantes, groups of men who took it on themselves to enforce the law on the frontier (Sp.)

village, Plains Indian villages consisted of lodges, property and people which were moved all together from place to place

wash-out, dried-out river-bed

Acknowledgements

We are grateful to the following for permission to reproduce copyright material:
Holt, Rinehart and Winston, Inc. for extracts from *America's Frontier Story: A Documentary History of Westward Expansion* edited by Martin Ridge and Ray Allen Billington.
Copyright © 1969 by Holt, Rinehart and Winston, Inc; University of Oklahoma Press for an extract from *Fifty Years on the Old Frontier*, by James H. Cook. New edition copyright 1957 by the University of Oklahoma Press and an extract from *We Pointed Them North*, by E. C. Abbott and Helena Huntington Smith. New edition copyright 1955 by the University of Oklahoma Press and Tro Essex Music Limited for the words of the following songs: "Get Along Little Dogies", "The Streets of Laredo" and "Billy the Kid".

For permission to reproduce illustrative material we are grateful to the following:

page

4 Beinecke Rare Book and Manuscript Library, Yale University, Western American Collection
7 Union Pacific Railroad (U.P.R.)
8 Out of copyright
12 Society of California Pioneers
12/13 U.P.R.
16 Library of Congress
19 U.P.R.
22 State Historical Society of Colorado
24 Utah State Historical Society
25 *left* Denver Rio Grande Western Railroad Company
   right Denver Public Library, Western History Department (D.P.L)
28 Illustrated London News
30 D.P.L.
32 D.P.L.
35 Mrs C Wade
38 Theodore Roosevelt Collection, Harvard College Library
39 Wayne Gard
41 Western History Collections, University of Oklahoma Library
46 Erwin E. Smith Collection, Library of Congress (E.E.S.C.)
47 Oklahoma Historical Society
48 Nebraska State Historical Society
51 University of Illinois Library
52 The Cattleman
52/53 E.E.S.C.

page

54 E.E.S.C.
55 E.E.S.C.
59 D.P.L.
60/1 D.P.L.
63 Kansas State Historical Society (K.S.H.S.)
65 *above* K.S.H.S.
65 *below* D.P.L.
67 D.P.L.
70 K.S.H.S.
75 Museum of New Mexico (M.N.M)
77 A.W. Jones, University of Illinois
78 M.N.M.
79 D.P.L.
81 D.P.L.
84 *above* U.S. Signal Corps from the Royal Archives (U.S.S.C)
84 *left* Smithsonian Institution, National Anthropological Archives, Bureau of American Ethnology Collection (S.I.)
84 *right* U.S.S.C.
87 S.I.
89 American Museum of Natural History
93 S.I.
97 Montana Stock Growers Association
98 D.P.L.
101 D.P.L.
103 National Film Archive
104 Culver Pictures Inc.